THE KARL MARX LIBRARY

EDITED AND TRANSLATED BY

SAUL K. PADOVER

Distinguished Service Professor of Political Science,
Graduate Faculty, New School for Social Research

ALREADY PUBLISHED

On Revolution

On America and the Civil War

On the First International

On Freedom of the Press and Censorship

On Religion

On Education, Women, and Children

TITLE IN PREPARATION

On History and People

Also by Saul K. Padover

THE REVOLUTIONARY EMPEROR: JOSEPH II

SECRET DIPLOMACY AND ESPIONAGE

(*with James Westfall Thompson*)

THE LIFE AND DEATH OF LOUIS XVI

JEFFERSON (a biography)

EXPERIMENT IN GERMANY

LA VIE POLITIQUE DES ÉTATS-UNIS

FRENCH INSTITUTIONS: VALUES AND POLITICS

THE GENIUS OF AMERICA

UNDERSTANDING FOREIGN POLICY

THE MEANING OF DEMOCRACY

THOMAS JEFFERSON AND THE FOUNDATIONS OF AMERICAN FREEDOM

· ·

Edited by Saul K. Padover

SOURCES OF DEMOCRACY: VOICES OF FREEDOM, HOPE AND JUSTICE

THOMAS JEFFERSON ON DEMOCRACY

THE COMPLETE JEFFERSON

THOMAS JEFFERSON AND THE NATIONAL CAPITAL

A JEFFERSON PROFILE

THE WRITINGS OF THOMAS JEFFERSON

THE COMPLETE MADISON (also titled: THE FORGING OF AMERICAN FEDERALISM)

THE WASHINGTON PAPERS

THE MIND OF ALEXANDER HAMILTON

WILSON'S IDEALS

THE LIVING UNITED STATES CONSTITUTION

CONFESSIONS AND SELF-PORTRAITS

THE WORLD OF THE FOUNDING FATHERS

NEHRU ON WORLD HISTORY

TO SECURE THESE BLESSINGS

On Education, Women, and Children

THE KARL MARX LIBRARY
VOLUME VI

On Education,
Women,
and Children

KARL MARX

ARRANGED AND EDITED, WITH AN
INTRODUCTION AND NEW TRANSLATIONS
by Saul K. Padover

McGraw-Hill Book Company

NEW YORK   ST. LOUIS   SAN FRANCISCO
DÜSSELDORF   LONDON   MEXICO   PANAMA
SYDNEY   TORONTO

123456789 BPBP 798765

Library of Congress Cataloging in Publication Data (Revised)
Marx, Karl, 1818–1883.
   The Karl Marx library.
   Includes bibliographies.
   CONTENTS: v. 1. On revolution.—v. 2. On America and the Civil
War.—v. 3. On the First International. [etc.]
   1. Socialism—Collected works.   I. Padover, Saul Kussiel, date ed.   II.
Title.
HX276.M2773   1972   335.43'08   78-172260
ISBN 0-07-048098-2
      0-07-048099-0 (pbk.)

Contents

Women and Children

Contents

Letters

Introduction
Marx: The Human Side

MARX's reputation as a particularly irascible curmudgeon is well established. In the course of his career, much of it polemical, he quarreled with, criticized, or ridiculed nearly all his friends and acquaintances, always excepting Frederick Engels. In speech and writing, his attacks on those he deemed to be personal or ideological—or merely unintelligent—opponents were unsparing. He was in the habit of assailing not only men's ideas but their motives, which he questioned sharply. His strictures, couched in terms of absolutes and expressed by an angry prophet with a total belief in his own rightness and righteousness, could not but create in the minds of contemporaries the image of a relentless hater.

Friend and foe acknowledged his brilliance but deplored his arrogance and ruthlessness. One of the earliest descriptions of Marx in action is by Pavel Vassilyevich Annenkov, a liberal Russian landowner who visited him in Brussels in 1846. Annenkov was invited to attend a small communist session where Wilhelm Weitling, an untutored German radical theorist not devoid of messianic delusions, was savagely castigated and intellectually destroyed by Marx. In later years, Annenkov, who liked and admired Marx, described the scene, which had left an indelible impression upon him:

> Marx himself was the type of man who is made up of energy, willpower, and unshakable conviction. . . . A mane of thick hair, hairy hands, his coat buttoned crookedly, he nevertheless looked like a man who had the right and the power to command respect. . . . His movements were clumsy, but bold and self-assured; his manners defied all the usual social conventions. But they were proud, with a tinge of contempt, and his sharp, metallic voice was remarkably

suited to the radical judgments he delivered on men and things. He spoke in nothing but imperatives, the words tolerating no opposition, penetrating everything he said in a harsh tone that jarred me almost painfully. The tone expressed his firm conviction of his mission to dominate men's minds and to prescribe laws for them.

Annenkov concluded acutely that in his eyes Marx personified a "democratic dictator."

A similar impression was recorded by Carl Schurz, who saw Marx two years after Annenkov. Schurz, a nineteen-year-old German revolutionist, visited Cologne in the summer of the revolutionary year 1848 and was anxious to meet the redoubtable Marx who, at the age of thirty, was editor of the radical *Neue Rheinische Zeitung*[1] and, as such, a power in the Rhineland. The meeting with Marx was a disappointment for the young man. In his *Reminiscences*, Schurz, who emigrated to the United States in 1852 and became an influential Republican politician, recalled Marx, to whom he was hostile, very much the way the friendly Annenkov did. Schurz wrote:

> The somewhat thickset man, with his broad forehead, his very black hair and beard, and his dark sparkling eyes, at once attracted general attention. . . . Marx's utterances were indeed full of meaning, logical and clear, but I have never seen a man whose bearing was so provoking and intolerable. To no opinion which differed from his, he accorded the honor of even a condescending consideration. Everyone who contradicted him he treated with abject contempt; every argument that he did not like he answered either with biting scorn . . . or with approbrious aspersions upon the motives of him who had advanced it. I remember most distinctly the cutting disdain with which he pronounced the word "bourgeois"; and as a "bourgeois," that is, as a detestable example of the deepest mental degeneracy, he denounced everyone that dared to oppose his opinions.

This dogmatism and intolerance of the opinions of others did not change with the years. Even where Marx was logical in his criticisms and profound in his comments, and he was often both, his harshness repelled many who would otherwise have been in sympathy with his ideas. As his parents and teachers recognized when he was still a boy, Marx tended toward extremism in his work and utterances. He had little gift for compromise and even less for self-criticism, and hence his tendency was to lash out without regard for the feelings of others.

Marx claimed that he did not care whether those whose ideas he found objectionable, or whose personalities he despised, loved or hated

---

1. See *Karl Marx on Freedom of the Press and Censorship*, Vol. IV of The Karl Marx Library (New York, 1974).

him. He had, in the words of his friend and follower, Wilhelm Lieb-knecht, a "sovereign contempt" for popularity, particularly for the applause of the common people, whose ideas he despised. "The masses," according to Liebknecht, "were to him a brainless crowd whose thoughts and feelings were furnished by the ruling class." Marx's Preface to the first German edition of *Capital* concluded with these words:

> Every opinion based on scientific criticism I welcome. As for the prejudices of so-called public opinion, to which I have never made concessions, now as before, the maxim of the great Florentine is mine:
>
> *Segui il tuo corso, e lascia dir le genti.*

He often used this quotation from Dante—"Follow your course and let the people say what they will"—in private conversation as well.

But the aloofness was a pose, assumed, probably unconsciously, as a shield against the catapults and shafts of a world which was out-rageous and hostile. Marx was frequently infuriated when the opinions he despised were aimed at him personally. In retaliation he was in the habit of seeking, recording, and eagerly repeating petty and malicious gossip about all those "bourgeois" and "*Knoten*" (boors, or louts), Marx's favorite pejoratives, who found him unlovable.

However, Marx, the angry radical and harsh critic in his public life and writings, was a very different sort of man in private. In his personal life, he was extraordinarily kind and generous and gay. Far from being a sour reformer or fanatic who detested joy and the pleasures of the flesh, Marx was a cheerful man in love with the good things of life. When he could afford it, he dressed elegantly and expensively, and in his middle years he wore a monocle with all the aplomb of an upperclass bourgeois gentleman. The monocle, suspended from the neck, went well with his finely tailored frock coats.

Marx cherished literature and music and the theater. When health and financial means allowed, he and his wife entertained guests with charm, gaiety, and amusing conversation. The home atmosphere, full of love and affection between the parents and the children, was often enlivened by *Lieder*, in the singing of which Marx joined, and hearty entertainment. At New Year's Eve parties, Marx, elegant and nimble, led his ladies in stately dances.

Always an optimist and even a romantic, Marx had a zest for merriment. A boon companion since his student days, he, like the even more convivial Frederick Engels, was capable of imbibing quantities of alcoholic liquids. As a native Rhinelander and lifelong devotee of French taste in all things, Marx had a particular fondness for wine.

"Since I come from a wine-growing region," he once wrote to François Lafargue, a Frenchman whose son Paul married Marx's daughter Laura, ". . . I know well how to appreciate the value of wine. I even agree a little with old Luther, who said that a man who does not love wine would never amount to anything much."

To Marx, wine was a pleasure and a panacea. Whenever he or members of his family, including the devoted, lifelong housekeeper, Helena Demuth ("Lenchen"), were sick, as they were with shocking frequency, they drank wine if they could get it. The doctors prescribed it as a medicine for practically everything. Wine was supposed to be a nepenthe for pain and a mitigator of fever. In the decades when Marx lived in desperate poverty in London he often asked Engels to send him not only money but also wine. Engels nearly always complied. The arrival of the hampers of wine, which the Marx family lined up admiringly in rows like "soldiers," was always a cause for celebration. When Engels visited London he and Marx would sometimes go reveling in pubs at night to the anger of Mrs. Marx. Herself a Rhinelander, she, too, savored wine, a taste which the Marx daughters also developed. But in addition to being a Rhinelander, Jenny Marx was a straitlaced German baroness who did not approve of excesses. When Marx and Engels were alone together they spent their time in sparkling talk and vinous conviviality.

Marx could be hilarious, for he had a keen and biting sense of humor, which he knew how to use. In his first critical political essay, "Remarks on the Latest Prussian Censorship Instruction," written in 1842,[2] he remarked: "I treat the ridiculous seriously when I treat it with ridicule." He loved humor, not merely for its own sake but also as ammunition against enemies. He quoted approvingly a stanza from his friend, the revolutionary German poet Georg Weerth:

Es gibt nichts Schönres auf der Welt
Als seine Feinde zu beissen,
Als ueber alle die plumpen Gesellen
Seine schlechten Witze zu reissen!

Freely translated, it reads:

There is nothing finer in the world
   Than to bite one's foes,
To inflict one's bad jokes
   On all those loutish blokes!*

---

2. See *Karl Marx On Freedom of the Press and Censorship*, Vol. IV of the Karl Marx Library, pp. 89–108.

* This poem and others in the Introduction have been translated by Saul K. Padover.

Marx's favorite poet was Heinrich Heine, probably Germany's foremost lyricist and certainly its greatest wit, whom he came to know and cherish when he lived in Paris in 1844. As a man of wide-ranging culture, at home in the Western world's great literature, much of which he read in the original languages, Marx frequently cited such authors as Cervantes, Dante, Goethe, Schiller, and Shakespeare. But it was Heine, whose sardonic humor he shared, whom he loved to quote when he wanted to make an amusing or barbed point. Thus, when he wished to show his disapproval of sentimentality, he referred to a satiric verse from Heine:

> *Ein Fräulein stand am Meere,*
> *Ihr war so weh und bang,*
> *Es grämte sie so sehre,*
> *Der Sonnenuntergang.*

Freely translated:

> A girl stood by the ocean shore
>   With pain and fear beset.
> Why is she so with worry sore?
>   Because the sun has set.

In reporting a dispute between two egoistic German socialists, Wilhelm Liebknecht and Johann Baptist von Schweitzer, Marx repeated the satiric lines from Heine's "Disputation" on a theological altercation between Father Joseph and Rabbi Judah:

> *Doch es will mich schier bedünken,*
> *das der Rabbi und der Mönch,*
> *dass sie beide stinken.*

Which may be rendered in English:

> Still, I truly think
> that the rabbi and the monk
> both together stink.

Marx's comments on men and events were often as sardonic as those of Heine. When Liebknecht, whom Marx occasionally criticized for political bumbling, became a father, he remarked: "Liebknecht has finally achieved something, namely, a young Liebknecht." At the news that his son-in-law, Dr. Paul Lafargue, had become a member of London's Royal College of Surgeons, Marx observed that the young doctor now had a "patent for the killing of men and beasts." A certain mediocre German journalist, Eugen Oswald, inspired Marx to remark drily that he was a "quite decent fellow, although he has not yet invented gunpowder." Referring to the two leading French·politicians of the era of Louis Philippe, Marx commented: "M. Guizot depicts M. Thiers and M. Thiers depicts M. Guizot as a traitor, and unfortunately they are both right." Of a famous German mystic, Marx said: "The shoemaker Jakob Boehme was a great philosopher. Many a professional philosopher is only a great shoemaker." At the news, in 1861, that an attempt had been made on the life of the Prussian king, Wilhelm I, Marx wondered about the would-be assassin: "How can any human being with ordinary sense risk his own life to kill a brainless jackass?" His comment on the crowned Autocrat of Russia, a country he despised and feared, was: "The Czar is great, God is greater, but the Czar is still young."

Some of his satiric barbs were self-directed. When he was reading final proofs of *Capital*, and was in great pain because of abscesses on his buttocks and scrotum, he remarked: "I hope the bourgeoisie will remember my carbuncles all the rest of their lives." Perhaps his wittiest remark was made shortly before his fiftieth birthday, when he found himself without worldly goods and, as always, financially dependent on Engels, to whom he wrote:

> In a few days I will be fifty. As that Prussian lieutenant once said to you, "Already twenty years in the service and still a lieutenant," so I can say: Half a century behind me and still a pauper! How right my mother was! "If only Karell had made capital instead!"

Making capital was alien to Marx. He who could write so profoundly and wisely about "*Geld*" and "*Gold*,"[4] had no money sense. Unlike Engels, he neither bothered to make money nor knew how to manage what he had when he had it. When in need, he would borrow desperately—sometimes at usurious rates as high as 20 percent—and he did this much too often. He was in debt most of his adult life. Perhaps as a reaction to his pennywise, hoarding, money-conscious Dutch mother, whom he did not like or respect, he showed his own improvidence and contempt for *Geld* by certain extravagances at times when the household was in despair over daily necessities.

A case in point is Marx's smoking. Until felled by chronic liver

---

3. This was how Marx's mother, a Dutchwoman who never really mastered the German language, pronounced "Karl."

4. See, for example, the section "Money" in *Economic and Philosophic Manuscripts of 1844*, where Marx uses a telling quotation from Shakespeare's *Timon of Athens* to illustrate the essence of money, this "glittering, precious gold" that has the overwhelming power to "make black white; foul, fair; wrong, right; base, noble; old, young; coward, valiant."

and lung ailments, and a cough that in the last decade of his life made sleep all but impossible without drugs, Marx was a heavy smoker. Although tubercular, rejected by the Prussian army because of his weak lungs and occasional blood-spitting, he began smoking as a student, to the dismay of his *Angst*-driven parents who were worried about his health. In fact, three or four of Marx's siblings died of tuberculosis. The parents' admonitions were in vain. Once out of the parental home, Marx shed their "bourgeois" habits and values and went his own independent way. Marx's father died in the despairing conviction that his gifted son, then a twenty-year-old student at the University of Berlin, was hopeless in his lack of practical sense and moderation.

Marx's smoking was, indeed, excessive, particularly for a man with his lung history. His smoking addiction was such that the atmosphere of the rooms in which he worked replicated a London fog—with a heavy admixture of sulfur, for Marx often forgot his pipe or cigar and kept on relighting it with "an incredible number of boxes of matches," according to his son-in-law Paul Lafargue. "When you enter Marx's room," a Prussian spy reported from London in the early 1850s, "smoke and tobacco fumes make your eyes water so much that for a moment you seem to be groping about in a cave." Marx's expenditure on cigars while writing *Capital* was so great that, he said, he doubted whether the book would ever sell enough copies to pay for them. But he developed a mock economic theory about his smoking. He found that if he bought cigars by the box, instead of piecemeal, he saved 1 shilling 6 pence per box. Since he smoked a box a day, he saved at least 547 shillings, or more than £45, a year! Thus, Marx said, the more he smoked the more money he saved. Q.E.D. Needless to say, Marx did not incorporate this particular theory of saving in his *Capital*.

Marx was not only an inveterate smoker but, like many a lusty male, also had a taste for the bawdy, which he culled from literature and history. In one letter to Engels, written a few months before his fiftieth birthday, Marx reported a couple of new carbuncles near his penis and quoted Mathurin Régnier's* verses on *chaude pisse* (hot piss) which he thought had never been "described more poetically anywhere else":

Mon cas, qui se lève et se hausse,
Bave d'une estrange façon;
Belle, vous fournistes la sausse,
Lors que je fournis le poisson.

---

* Mathurin Régnier (1573-1613), a French satirist, was the author of *Epigrammes*.

Las! si ce membre eut l'arrogance
De fouiller trop les lieux sacrez,
Qu'on luy pardonne son offence,
Car il pleure assez ses péchez.

My dingus, which rises and gets higher,
Foams in a strange fashion;
Beauty, you furnish the sauce,
while I furnish the fish.

Alack! if this member had the arrogance
To rummage in sacred places,
His offense should be pardoned
Because he weeps enough over his sins.

Then Marx went on to quote Régnier on the function of the male
membrum:

Fluxion D'Amour
L'amour est une affection
Qui, par les yeux, dans le cœur entre
Et, par la forme de fluxion,
S'éxcoule par le bas du ventre.

The Fluxion of Love
Love is an emotion
That enters the heart through the eyes,
And, in the form of a fluxion,
Flows through the bottom of the belly.

Lisette tuée par Régnier
Lisette, à qui l'on faisait tort,
Vint à Régnier tout éplorée,
Je te pry, donne moi la mort
Que j'ay tant de fois desirée!
Luy, ne la refusant en rien,
Tire son . . . , vous m'entendez bien,
Et dedans le ventre la frappe.
Elle, voulant finir ses jours
Luy dit: Mon cœur pousse toujours,
De crainte que je n'en réchappe.
Régnier, las de la secourir,
Craignant une second plainte,
Lui dit: Hastez-vous de mourir
Car mon poignard n'a plus de pointe.

Lisette Slain by Régnier
Lisette, who has been wronged,
Comes to Régnier all in tears,

> I beg you, give me the death
> That I have wished for so many times!
> He, refusing her nothing,
> Pulls out his . . . , you know what I mean,
> And strikes inside her belly.
> She, desiring to end her days,
> Says to him: My heart always beats
> With the fear that I will not get out alive.
> Régnier, tired of succoring her,
> Fearing a second plea,
> Says to her: Hasten to die,
> Because my dagger no longer has a point.

Marx repeated this metaphor of sex satisfaction and death in a story about a thoroughly healthy father confessor who, after spending twenty-four hours in a Russian convent, came out dead. "The nuns rode him to death," he wrote, and added a French pun: father confessors, of course, "do *not enter* every day."

In a similar spirit, Marx once expressed his inability to supply a friend with his written works. When Nicolai Frantzevich Danielson, the Russian co-translator of *Capital*, asked Marx for his earlier writings, the latter replied that much as he would like to oblige, he simply did not possess such a collection, and cited a French expression: "*la plus belle fille de France ne peut donner que ce qu'elle a*"—the prettiest girl in France cannot give any more than what she has. In another vein of bawdiness, he wrote[5] that Empress Eugénie, wife of Napoleon III, whom he detested, suffered from the affliction of farting in public, a tympoptano mania" which she could not control, and again he fell back on the French language, in which he was about as fluent as he was in German: "*Ce n'est qu'un petit bruit, un murmure, un rien: mais enfin, vous savez que les Français ont le nez au plus petit vent.*" ('Tis but a small noise, a murmur, a nothing; but, after all, you know the French have a nose for the smallest wind.) Funnier than the comment on Eugénie's "tympoptano mania" was Marx's report, in the *New-York Daily Tribune* (September 30, 1854), on the Spanish Queen Christina and her lover, the Spanish toreador José Muñoz Benavente (a) Pucheta:

> The relation of Christina and this same Muñoz can only be understood from the answer given by Don Quixote to Sancho Panza's question why he was in love with such a low country wench as his Dulcinea, when he could have princesses at his feet: "A lady," answered the worthy knight, "surrounded by a host of high-bred, rich and witty followers, was asked why she took for her lover a simple

---

5. See letter to Adolf Cluss, March 25, 1853.

peasant. 'You must know,' said the lady, 'that for the office for which I use him he possesses more philosophy than Aristotle himself.' "

Marx had a genuine affection and esteem for women. He treated his own wife and daughters not only with tenderness but also with respect for their minds. His confidence in Mrs. Marx's judgment and wisdom was such that he consulted her about everything, including political ideas. This trust he also extended to his housekeeper, Lenchen, whose opinions he sought and heeded. As for his own three daughters, he raised them to be women of culture and intellectual independence. They, in turn, appreciating the respect he showed them as personalities, admired and adored him.

Marx was outraged at the mistreatment and exploitation of women in the capitalist system, as can be seen in the eloquent passages from *Capital* included in this volume. Despite his public fierceness, he was a man of immense compassion—his daughter Eleanor ("Tussy") referred to his kindness and patience as "really sublime"—easily moved to pity for the weak and oppressed, foremost especially among them being women and children. Wife beating, then common in England, particularly among the poorer classes, filled him with such rage that, according to a friend, he would have gladly flogged such an offender "to the point of death."

His instinctive compassion for women once got him in trouble in London. He was riding in an omnibus with Wilhelm Liebknecht when he heard a shrill female voice screaming "Murder! Murder!" At this sound of the strumpet Marx leaped from the carriage and, followed by a reluctant Liebknecht, rushed to the rescue of the lady, who, it happened, was a drunken wife whom her husband was trying to get home. As Marx, obviously an alien in appearance and speaking broken English, barged in, the wrangling couple, instantly reconciled, turned furiously on the swarthy intruder, the intoxicated woman going after his provocatively magnificent beard. A crowd soon joined in the attack on the "damned foreigners," who were finally rescued by two burly constables. That incident taught Marx not to be so impulsively chivalrous in the future.

His own marriage had its roots in a passionate romance, à la some of the German novels of the period. He and Jenny von Westphalen, four years his senior, had met when they were children, fallen in love while at school, and became secretly engaged before he went off to the university at the age of seventeen. He was then in emotional turmoil, unmoored by a love that seemed to have no practical future. Jenny was not only considered to be "the most beautiful girl in Trier," but a baroness accustomed to a life of ease and comfort. How could

young Marx, romantic, impractical, and without wealth, ever hope
to support an aristocratic wife? Under the *Sturm und Drang* of his
situation, young Marx, at the University of Berlin, sought refuge in
writing poetry. His ambition, despite his father's urgings to become a
lawyer, was to be a literary man, a dramatist and poet like Lessing.
Poetry, he wrote to his father, was "my heaven, my art" and constant
"companion." The various stresses which he suffered at this time
finally pushed him to a nervous breakdown.

By November 1836 the eighteen-and-a-half-year-old Marx had
filled three notebooks with poems, entitling one of them *Buch de Liebe*
(Book of Love). It contained thirty-five lyrics, ballads, and sonnets,
and was dedicated to "*Meiner teueren, ewiggeliebten* (My precious,
eternally beloved) Jenny v. Westphalen."

The poetry was derivative and not very inspired, as Marx, whose
critical sense rarely abandoned him for long, was soon to realize.
The rhyming drivel can be judged from the "Final Sonnet to Jenny"
in the *Buch der Liebe*:

> *Eines muss ich Dir, mein Kind, noch sagen,*
> *Fröhlich schliesst mein Abschiedsang den Rhein,*
> *Denn die letzen Silberwellen schlagen,*
> *Sich in Jennys Hauche Klang zu leihn,*
> *So wird kühn durch Felsensprung und Ragen,*
> *Lauf durch Flutenfall und Hain,*
> *Fort der Stundenlauf des Lebens schlagen,*
> *Zur Vollendung sich in Dir zu weihn.*
>
> *Kühn gehüllt in weiten Glutgewanden,*
> *Lichtverklärt das stolzbehob'ne Herz,*
> *Herrschend losgesagt von Zwang und Banden,*
> *Tret' ich festen Schritt's durch weit Räume,*
> *Schmett're vor Dein Antlitz hin den Schmerz,*
> *Und zum Lebensbaum entsprühn die Träume!*

This may be rendered in free translation thus:

> One thing more, my child, I must tell:
> Joyously I end with this song of farewell;
> For the last silvery waves so roll
> As on Jenny's breath to find their soul,
> Leaping boldly over rock and tower,
> Running through rising flood and shower,
> While the hours with life pulsate
> Their fulfillment in you to consecrate.
>
> Boldly envelop'd in ardor's mantle wide,
> The luminous heart lifted with pride,

Triumphantly freed from force and strain
I tread firmly through the spacious terrain,
Pain shattering before your visage that gleams,
And from life's tree sprout the dreams!"

In later years, Marx and Jenny laughed when they reread his juvenile concoctions.

But their young love was serious indeed. When their engagement became known, both their families reacted adversely. The von Westphalens were aristocrats, occupying high government positions (Jenny's half-brother, Ferdinand Otto Wilhelm von Westphalen, was Prussian Minister of Interior for eight years). The Marxes, recent converts to Christianity, were descendants of rabbis, and, though reasonably prosperous, had no social pretensions. But fundamentally the opposition of both families was based on economic considerations. Neither family could see how Marx, a young man without means, could support a family. Even if he became a lawyer, as his dying father urged him to do, it would take him many years before he could earn enough to set up and maintain a household. Jenny was attractive and desirable and much older than Karl; the family asked how long she could afford to wait. Karl's widowed mother, for her part, disliked the whole situation. What business did her "Karell," the gifted oldest son whom she expected to be a good moneymaker and provider, have getting involved with the town's aristocracy? She was a poorly educated, practical *Hausfrau*, suspicious of the likes of the von Westphalens, who, indeed, snubbed her after her husband's death.

The family opposition only strengthened Jenny's and Karl's love and hardened their determination, for they were both iron-willed individuals. Karl, at the university, pursued his literary and philosophic studies, ignoring all practical considerations; Jenny, at home, resisted every pressure to the point of frequent and grave illnesses. Like a latter-day version of Jacob and Rachel, they waited for seven years before they could marry. The beautiful Jenny's passion for the swarthy Karl, one of the homeliest boys in Trier, whom she addressed as her "*Schwarzwildchen*" (Darling Wild Boar) and "lord and master," all but engulfed her:

Karl, Karl, how I love you! . . . Everything I bear in my heart, all my senses and thoughts, everything past, present, and future, is only an utterance, a sign, a tone, and when it rings, it means this only: I love you inexpressibly, limitlessly, immeasurably. . . .

His own intimate letters, like most of hers to him, no longer exist; they were largely destroyed by Marx's prudish daughter Laura Lafargue after her father's death. But all available evidence indicates that he shared Jenny's passion, physically and emotionally. In one of his preserved letters, to Arnold Ruge, he wrote:

> Without any romanticism, I can assure you that I am head over heels seriously in love. I have been engaged now for seven years, and my fiancée has had to fight for me the hardest battles, which practically undermined her health, partly with her pietistic-conservative relatives, for whom the "Lord in Heaven" and the "Lord in Berlin" are equal objects of worship, partly with my own family.

Some two months after writing this letter, on June 19, 1843, Karl Marx, twenty-five-year-old Doctor of Philosophy, and Jenny von Westphalen, twenty-nine-year-old spinster, were married in an Evangelical church, although he was no longer a believing Christian. The only family member present was Frau von Westphalen, Jenny's widowed mother. The rest of the von Westphalens, as well as Marx's widowed mother and his siblings and other relatives, were pointedly absent. The disapproval of their families did not prevent the newly-weds from enjoying a blissful honeymoon in Rheinpfalz, Switzerland. Recalling those "golden days," Marx once quoted—in a newspaper article on politics![6]—a few wistful lines from one of his (and his father's) favorite German poets:

O zarte Sehnsucht, süsses Hoffen,
Der ersten Liebe goldne Zeit!
Das Auge sieht den Himmel offen,
Es schwelgt das Herz in Seligkeit—
O dass sie ewig grünen bleibe,
Die schöne Zeit der jungen Liebe.[7]

Marx himself, who had started his writing career as a poet, translated this as follows:

Oh, tender longings, sweet hopes,
golden time of first love!
The eye sees heavens open,
the heart luxuriates in bliss.
Oh, that it could bloom forever,
that golden time of young love!

The marital bliss did not, of course, bloom forever, but the marriage lasted thirty-eight years, until Jenny's death. When she died, something in Marx died with her; he survived her by hardly more than

---

6. Marx, "Prussia. The New Ministry," in *New-York Daily Tribune*, November 24, 1858.
7. From Friedrich von Schiller, *Das Lied von der Glocke.*

a year. Their married life had been one of cruel economic hardship and deep companionship. Jenny's self-sacrifice for the husband she adored, and of whom she was always jealous where other women were concerned, was total. So was her devotion to him and his cause. She held the family together in the most desperate circumstances and sustained Marx with her courage and keen intelligence. He, who depended upon her for everything, including literary and political opinions, in turn reciprocated her devotion and love. Although he strayed occasionally, Jenny was the only woman in his life. Thirteen years after their marriage, Marx was still capable of writing to his forty-two-year-old wife a love letter imbued with remarkable youthful passion:[8]

> *My heart's beloved:*
> I am writing you again, because I am alone and because it troubles me always to have a dialogue with you in my head, without your knowing anything about it or hearing it or being able to answer. Poor as your photograph is, it does perform a service for me, and I now understand how even the "black Madonna," the most disgraceful portrait of the Mother of God, could find indestructible admirers. . . . Those black Madonna pictures have never been more kissed, looked at, and adored than your photograph, which . . . absolutely does not reflect your darling, sweet, kissable, "*dolce*" face. . . . I have you vividly before me, and I carry you on my hands, and I kiss you from head to foot, and I fall on my knees before you, and I groan: "Madame, I love you. . . ."

He went on to say that his momentary absence (he was visiting Engels in Manchester) only revealed how great his love for her was and how it energized and regenerated his whole existence as a man. He concluded:

> There are actually many females in the world, and some among them are beautiful. But where could I find again a face whose every feature, even every wrinkle, is a reminder of the greatest and sweetest memories of my life? Even my endless pains, my irreplaceable losses, I read in your sweet countenance, and I kiss away the pain when I kiss your sweet face. "Buried in her arms, awakened by her kisses"—namely, in your arms and by your kisses, and I grant the Brahmins and Pythagoras their doctrine of regeneration and Christianity its doctrine of resurrection.

Marx was a vigorous male, uninhibited in his sexual fervor, an ardency which the sensuous Jenny, despite frequent breakdowns of her health, clearly shared. They procreated as if children had no economic

---

8. See Marx to Jenny, Manchester, June 21, 1856.

consequences. Their first child—also named Jenny, or "Jennychen," who became Marx's favorite—was born in 1844, within a year of their marriage. Thenceforth, Jenny was pregnant almost annually until her menopause. She gave birth to seven children, four of whom died in infancy or in childhood. All the children were born in exile—Paris, Brussels, London—when Marx had little financial means and no paying profession except journalism, the income from which was meager and uncertain. In a letter to Engels, whose continuous financial hand-outs saved the Marx family from starvation in England, he referred to himself as a "strong-loined paterfamilias" whose marriage was "more productive" than his earnings. The fecund Marx also sired a son, Freddy Demuth, by his housekeeper, Helena Demuth, and refused to acknowledge the paternity, for fear that it would break up his marriage. Jenny and everybody else went along with the fiction that Engels, a gay and elegant cavalier who lived with a mistress in Manchester, where he was a gentleman businessman and fox hunter, was Freddy's father. He accepted this role of putative father as a favor to Marx, his closest friend. In later years, when Marx was away from home he flirted with other women, unbeknown to the fiercely jealous Jenny. Some of the middle-aged Marx's correspondence with his Dutch cousin, Antoinette ("Nannette") Philips, who was nineteen years his junior, are close to being outright love letters.

Marx's extraordinary love for children, his own and others, is the most luminous feature of his character. He was, a friend who knew him intimately said of him, "a child among children." When out walking on Hampstead Heath he would stop and play with children, who responded easily to the bushy-bearded kindly stranger. While disapproving of adult mendicants, Marx could not resist child beggars, particularly ragged little girls, whose hair he would stroke and for whom he would empty his pockets of small change. Although a materialist with an antipathy for all religion, including Christianity,[9] Marx used to say that what he liked most about Christ was His great love for children.

Marx adored his own children. He was, in turn, idolized by them. It was for him a special tragedy that his two sons died young; Heinrich Guido, nicknamed "Föxchen" (all the children had nicknames), as a one-year-old infant, and Edgar, "Musch," at the age of eight. The death of Musch, a bright and lively boy who filled the household with booming songs and who died in his father's arms, left Marx shattered and unconsolable. Years after Musch died (in 1855) in Soho, Marx could not pass the neighborhood without shuddering at the terrible memory of the loss of his son.

---

9. See *Karl Marx on Religion*, Vol. V of The Karl Marx Library.

To his surviving three daughters, Marx was not a Germanic authoritarian papa, but a loving playmate and inspiring teacher. On Sundays, in good weather, he and the whole family would march to Hampstead Heath, where they would picnic and romp. Marx would play the "maddest and merriest" games with the children, among them walking on all fours, pretending he was a horse, which the children gleefully rode. After a hearty meal—roast veal, bread, cheese, fruit, savories, tea or ginger beer, carried to the Heath by Lenchen in a hamper—they would walk home tired but exhilarated, the children singing folksongs, the others, including Papa Marx, belting out *Lieder* such as "*O Strassburg, O Strassburg, du wunderschöne Stadt!*"

Marx was also a superb storyteller with a fertile imagination. Even as a boy in Trier he used to invent amusing stories to mollify his siblings after he had bullied them. In London, as he walked with the children he would often entertain them with fairy tales by the mile. When they wanted more, they would beg him: "Tell us another mile." His youngest daughter, Eleanor ("Tussy"), recalled how she specially loved the story of Hans Roeckle, which Marx spun out for months and months and which never came to an end. Roeckle was a magician who had all kinds of toys in his shop: wooden men and women, giants and dwarfs, kings and queens, masters and apprentices, birds and animals as numerous as in Noah's ark. Roeckle, always in need of money, had to sell his most beautiful things, piece by piece, to the devil. But after many adventures, they would always come back to Roeckle's shop, and a new cycle of stories would begin. "Some of these stories," Eleanor wrote, "were gruesome and hair-raising . . . others were funny, but all were told with an inexhaustible reservoir of inventiveness, fantasy and humor."

The three Marx daughters, who inherited intelligence from their father and beauty from their mother, were given an excellent education. They were exposed to literature and political ideas quite early in life. Marx read to his children all of Homer, the *Niebelungenlied*, *Don Quixote*, *A Thousand and One Nights*. "Shakespeare," Eleanor recalls, "was our house bible; at the age of six I knew whole scenes from Shakespeare by memory." On her sixth birthday she was given her first novel, Frederick Marryat's *Peter Simple*, and later books by James Fenimore Cooper and Sir Walter Scott, which Marx, an avid novel reader in several languages, read and discussed with his daughters. Their education also included music lessons, even though Marx could not afford a piano, singing, drawing, and languages. The household sometimes went hungry to pay for the girls' tuition, which was frequently in arrears, but the otherwise radical Marx was determined that his daughters have a respectable bourgeois upbringing. The girls grew up to be world-minded and multilingual. In 1861, when

Jennychen was seventeen, Laura sixteen, and Eleanor six, their mother wrote about them to a German friend, Louise Weydemeyer, residing in St. Louis, Missouri:

> They are completely at home in English, and they know French well. In Italian they understand Dante, they also read some Spanish; only in German is there a hitch, and although I make every effort to give them a German lesson now and then, still they manage to parry it, and my authority here does not carry very far.

In Marx's view, education should be a shared experience between parents and their offspring, and not a forcible imposition of discipline. "Children," he used to say, "should educate their parents." Such a relationship enriches education and assures mutual respect and love. Marx's own daughters, to whom, in the words of one of them, he was an "ideal friend," rewarded him with lifelong devotion.

When Marx became a grandfather, he lavished the same love on his grandchildren as he had on his own offspring. His special favorite was his oldest grandson, Jean Laurent Frederick ("Johnny"), the son of his daughter Jennychen and Charles Longuet, a French socialist. Johnny was born in 1876 and lived until 1938. When Johnny got to be three or four years old, he was sent to London to be with his grandparents several times a year. Little Johnny could do anything he liked with his doting grandpapa In the small gravel-and-grass garden of the Marx's Maitland Park Road cottage Johnny would make his *grandpère* go down on all fours, climb on his back, and shout in two languages: "Go on! *Plus vite!* Hurrah!" The white-haired Marx, then in his sixties, would meekly trot along, while the little rascal yelled: "You naughty horse! *En avant!*" Grandpa Marx, sweat pouring down his face, was entranced. Until his death in 1883, at the age of sixty-five, Marx was insatiable for the presence of his grandchildren and indefatigable in his love for them.

His deep affection for children explains why, in his *Capital*, he devoted so much detail to their exploitation in shops and factories. The brutal abuse of the young and weak in capitalist England filled him with outrage.

Marx's continuing indignation at widespread suffering was thus rooted in his own basic humanity, his easily aroused compassion for the downtrodden, the victims of what he considered to be an evil social system. His anger at injustice may be viewed as the fuel which propelled his polemical writings and enforced his social-economic theories.

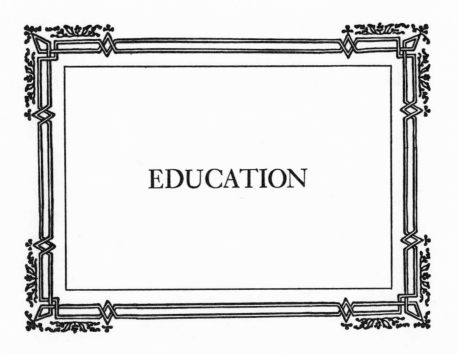

EDUCATION

Reflections of a Young Man on
Choosing an Occupation

Karl Marx's examination essay, written between August 10 and 16, 1835, before his graduation on September 24, 1835, from the Trier *Gymnasium*

NATURE itself has assigned to the animal a sphere of activity in which it is to move, and the animal does so contentedly, without striving beyond it or even knowing that there is any other. To man, too, the Deity gave a general goal, that of ennobling mankind and himself, but left it up to him to seek the means by which this could be achieved; it left it up to him to choose the position in society most appropriate to him and from which he can best elevate both himself and society.

This choice is a great privilege over other creatures, but at the same time an act which can destroy a man's whole life, frustrate all his plans, and make him unhappy. To weigh this choice seriously is surely the first duty of a youth who is at the beginning of his career and who does not want to leave the most important concerns to chance.

Every person has a goal which appears great, at least to himself, and is great when the deepest convictions, the innermost voice of the heart, calls it so, because the Deity never leaves the earthling entirely without a guide; it speaks softly but surely.

This voice, however, is easily drowned out, and what we thought to be inspiration may have been the creation of a moment and can also be destroyed in a moment. Our imagination is perhaps inflamed, our senses excited; phantoms flutter before our eyes and eagerly we rush to the goal, which we presume that the Deity itself has shown us. But what we ardently press to our breast soon repels us, and we see our whole existence destroyed.

We must, therefore, seriously ask ourselves whether we are really inspired for a vocation, whether an inner voice approves of it, or whether the enthusiasm was a deception, that what we had thought to be a vocation from the Deity was only self-deceit. But how else can we manage to recognize this than by searching the source of our inspiration?

Greatness glitters, glitter stirs ambition, and ambition can easily bring forth the inspiration, or what we thought to be such; but when the fury of ambition tempts, reason can no longer restrain it, and man tumbles where his vehement impulse urges him; he no longer chooses his position, but rather chance and illusion determine it.

Then we are not called to the position in which we can most excel; it is not the one which in the long succession of years during which we may perhaps occupy it will never tire us, diminish our zeal, or cool our enthusiasm, but, instead, we shall see our wishes unfulfilled, our ideas unsatisfied, and we shall grumble against the Deity and curse mankind.

But not only ambition can stimulate a sudden inspiration for a position; we may also perhaps have embellished it with our fantasies, embellished it to reach the highest point that life can offer. We have not analyzed it, not considered the entire burden, the great responsibility. it puts upon us; we have seen it only from a distance, and distance deceives.

In this, our own reason cannot be the counselor, for it is supported neither by experience nor by profound observation, while it is deceived by emotion and blinded by fantasy. To whom, then, shall we turn for support when our reason forsakes us?

Our heart calls upon our parents, who have already walked the path of life and experienced the severity of fate.

And if our inspiration still persists, if we still love the position for which we believe ourselves to be called after we have tested it cooly, perceived its burdens, and learned about its encumbrances—then may we take it up, then we are deceived neither by the inspiration nor by the rush of overeagerness.

But we cannot always avail ourselves of the position to which we believe we are called; our relations in society, to some extent, have already begun before we are able to determine them.

Even our physical nature often confronts us menacingly, and no one dare to mock its rights!

We may, to be sure, rise above it, but then we sink all the faster; we then dare to construct a building on rotten foundations, and our entire life becomes an unfortunate struggle between the intellectual and the physical. If, however, one cannot subdue the fighting elements inside oneself, how, then, can one stand up against the wildest urges of life; how can one act calmly? Only out of calmness can great and beautiful deeds emerge; it is the only soil on which ripe fruits thrive.

Although we cannot work for long, and rarely joyfully, with a physical nature not appropriate for our position, there always arises the thought of sacrificing our own welfare to duty, of acting with weakness and yet with firmness. Nevertheless, if we have chosen a position for which we have no talents, we shall be unable to fill it worthily and shall soon recognize with shame our incompetence and tell ourselves that we are a useless creature, a member of society who cannot fill his post. The most natural consequence, then, is self-contempt, and what feeling is more painful and less capable of being cured by anything the outside world may offer? Self-contempt is a serpent that always ragingly gnaws in one's breast, sucks out the heart's lifeblood, and mixes it with the venom of hatred for humanity and despair.

A deception about our aptitude for a position, which we have examined closely, is a lapse which falls back upon us vengefully, and even though it may not be censured by the outside world, it provokes in our breast a pain more terrible than any the latter may cause.

After we have weighed everything regarding the position permitted by our condition in life, we may take up the one that guarantees us the greatest dignity, which is based on ideas of whose truth we are completely convinced, which offers the largest field to work for humanity and enables us to approach the universal goal for which every position is only a means: perfection.

Dignity is what elevates man most, what lends a higher nobility to all his acts and all his endeavors, what permits him to stand irreproachably, admired by the multitude and above it.

Only that position can impart dignity in which we do not appear as servile tools but rather create independently in our own sphere; only that position can impart dignity which requires no reprehensible acts, reprehensible even in appearance—a position which the best person can take up with noble pride. The position that guarantees this most is not always the most exalted, but it is always the superior one.

Just as a position without dignity debases us, so also we surely succumb to the burden of one which rests on ideas we later recognize as false.

Then we see no help except in self-deception, and what a desperate rescue is this that guarantees self-betrayal!

Positions which do not take hold of life but deal, rather, with abstract truths are the most dangerous for a youth whose principles are not yet matured, whose conviction is not yet firm and unshakable, although at the same time they may appear to be the loftiest when they have taken root deep in the breast and when we can sacrifice life and all strivings for the ideas thus held.

They can make happy the one who is called for them; but they destroy the one who takes them overhastily, without reflection, on the spur of the moment.

But the high opinion we have of the ideas on which our vocation is based imparts to us a higher standpoint in society, enlarges our own dignity, makes our actions unshakable.

Whoever chooses a position which he esteems highly will recoil from making himself unworthy of it; he will, therefore, act nobly because his position in society is noble.

The main principle, however, which must guide us in the selection of a position is the welfare of mankind, our own consummation. One should not think that these two interests are in hostile conflict and that the one must destroy the other, but, rather, that human nature is such that man's fulfillment can be attained only when he works for the perfection and welfare of his fellow men.

If a person works only for himself he can perhaps be a famous scholar, a great sage, a distinguished poet, but never a fulfilled, genuinely great man.

History calls those the greatest men who, while working for the universal, ennobled themselves; experience praises as the most happy the one who has made the most people happy; religion itself teaches us that the ideal, striven for by all, is the one who sacrificed himself for humanity, and who would dare contest such claims?

When we have chosen the position in which we can do most for humanity, burdens cannot bow us down, because they are only sacrifices for mankind. Then we experience no meager, narrow, egoistic joy, but our happiness belongs to millions, our deeds live on quietly but ever actively, and our ashes will be moistened by the glowing tears of noble men.

His Intellectual Travail

Karl Marx, Letter to his father
NOVEMBER 10, 1837*

Dear Father:

There are moments in life which stand as landmarks, terminating the past and at the same time pointing firmly (in) a new direction.

At such a point of transition we feel compelled to contemplate, with the eagle eye of thought, the past and the present, in order to arrive at a true awareness of our actual situation. Indeed, world history itself loves such a retrospect, seeming to move backwards and to stand still, whereas in reality it leans back in the armchair to understand itself and to penetrate intellectually its own act, the act of the mind.

The individual, however, becomes lyrical in such moments, because metamorphosis is partly swan song, partly overture to a great new poem that tries to gain shape amidst the hazy yet brilliant colors; and yet we should erect a monument to what we have already experienced, so that it should regain in sensibility what it has lost in action; and where could we find a more sacred abode than in the hearts of our parents, the most indulgent judges, the most intimate participants, the sun of love whose fire warms our innermost strivings! What better way is there to correct, and to receive forgiveness for, what is displeasing and blameworthy in our character, than to look at it as an essentially necessary condition? In what other way can one escape the reproach of having a twisted heart than by ascribing it as much to adverse luck and to aberration of spirit as to anything else?

If now, at the end of a year spent here, I review the events of that period, and, in doing so, dear Father, answer the affectionate letter you

---

* This is the only letter preserved from Marx's youth.

wrote me from Ems, I take the liberty of examining my situation and, in general, my view of life, which I consider an expression of reflections taking shape from many sources—science, art, and private endeavors.

When I left home, a new world had opened up for me, one of love and, at first, a love drunk with longing and empty of hope. Even the trip to Berlin, which overwise would have enchanted me to the highest degree, would have inspired me to contemplate nature, and inflamed me to a joy of living, left me cold, and indeed, depressed me considerably. For the rocks I saw were no steeper, no bleaker than the sensations of my soul, the broad cities no livelier than my blood, the restaurant tables no more overloaded with indigestible food than the contents of my imagination, and, finally, art itself, which was not as beautiful as Jenny.

Upon arrival in Berlin, I broke with all existing connections, paid rare visits and then only with reluctance, and sought to immerse myself in science and art.

In my state of mind then, lyrical poetry was necessarily the first, at least the most pleasant, project I embarked upon, but, in accord with my position and previous development, it was purely idealistic. An equally remote otherworld, such as my love, became my heaven, my art. Everything real became blurred, and the vague had no boundaries. Attacks on the present, wide and shapeless feelings, nothing natural, everything constructed out of the blue, the complete opposite of that which is and which should be, rhetorical reflections instead of poetic ideas, but perhaps also a certain warmth of feeling and a striving for vigor—all this characterizes the poems in the first three volumes I sent to Jenny. The whole horizon of longing, which sees no limit, assumes various forms and turns "versifying" into "width."

Poetry, however, was to be merely a companion; I had to study law and I felt above all an urge to grapple with philosophy. The two were so closely connected that I studied Heineccius,[1] Thibaut,[2] and the sources uncritically and in schoolboy fashion; thus, for example, I translated the first two books of the Pandect into German and tried to work out a philosophy of law while studying law. By way of introduction, I preceded it with some metaphysical propositions and then continued this unfortunate opus up to public law, a work of almost three hundred pages.

Above all, I was troubled by the same contradictions between the Is and the Ought that is characteristic of Idealism, and this led me to make the following hopelessly inaccurate divisions: First, the meta-

---

1. Johann Gottlieb Heineccius, *Elementa iuris civilis secundum ordinem Pandectarum* (Amsterdam, 1728).

2. Anton Friedrich Justus Thibaut, *System des Pandekten-Rechts*, Vols. I–II (Jena, 1803–05).

physics of law, as I gratuitously termed it, that is, the principles, reflections, and definitions of concepts, divorced from all real law and all real forms of law, as is the case with Fichte,[3] but in my case more modern and less substantial. This—the unscholarly form of mathematical dogmatism, where the subject circles around the matter, reasons to and fro, without the matter itself forming into something rich and alive—obstructed an understanding of the truth from the outset. The triangle leads the mathematician to construct and to demonstrate; it remains a mere idea in space, it does not develop into anything else; it has to be set beside something else to assume different positions, and these, when juxtaposed to related ones, yield different relationships and truths. On the other hand, in all concrete expressions in the living world of ideas, such as Law, the State, Nature, and all of philosophy, the object itself has to be observed in its development, arbitrary divisions must not be intruded, and the reason of the thing itself must evolve within its own contending self and find there its own unity.

As a second part, there followed the philosophy of law, that is, according to the opinion I then held about the development of ideas in positive Roman law, as if positive law in its intellectual evolution (I do not mean in its purely finite definitions) could exist at all apart from the shape of the concept of law, which, after all, the first part should have included!

In addition, I had divided that part into formal and substantive theory of law, of which the first was meant to outline the pure form of the system in its progression and context, its structure and scope; whereas the second part was to deal with content and the merging of form into content. There is one error which I share with Herr von Savigny, as I was to discover later when I read his erudite work on property—with the difference that what he called formal definition was something "to find the place which this or the other doctrine has in the (hypothetical) Roman system," and the material definition was that which is "the doctrine of the positive which the Romans attributed to a concept defined in this manner";—I, on the other hand, considered form as the architectonics required in the formulation of a concept, and matter as the quality required of these forms. The error was that I believed the one could and should develop independently of the other, and thus I did not arrive at true form but merely constructed a writing desk with drawers which I later filled with sand.

Concept is, after all, the mediating element between form and content. In any philosophical treatise on law, therefore, the one must be contained in the other; indeed, form should be but the continuation of

---

3. Johann Gottlieb Fichte, *Grundlage des Naturrechts nach Prinzipien der Wissenschaftslehre* (Jena and Leipzig, 1796).

content. Thus I arrived at a division that made for simple and super-
ficial classification only, while the spirit of law and its truth were
obscured by it. The whole body of law fell into contract and non-
contract elements. For better illustration, I take the liberty of present-
ing here the schema up to the division of the *jus publicum*, which has
also been treated in the formal part.

I	II
jus privatum	*jus publicum*

I. *jus privatum*
a. Conditional, contractual private law
b. Unconditional, noncontractual private law

   A. *Conditional, contractual private law*
     a. Personal law
     b. Property law
     c. Personal reality law

a. Personal law
I. Out of encumbered contract
II. Out of assured contract
III. Out of charitable contract

   I. Out of encumbered contract
2. Social contract (*societas*)
3. Hiring-out contract (*locatio conductio*)
   3. *Locatio conductio*
     1. Insofar as it relates to services (*operae*)
       a. Real *locatio conductio* (not meant to include
         Roman house- or farm-lease laws)
       b. *mandatum*
     2. Insofar as it relates to the right of use (*usus rei*)
       a. Ground: *ususfructus* (but not also in the purely
         Roman sense)
       b. Dwellings: *habitatio*

   II. *Out of the assured contract*
1. Separation or adjustment contract
2. Insurance contract

   III. *Out of charitable contract*
     2. *Consent contract*
1. *fidejussio* (surety)
2. *negotiorum gestio* (conducting business without man-
date)

3. *Donation contract*
1. *donatio* (gift)
2. *gratiae promissum* (promises of favor)

b. *Property law*
I. *Out of encumbered contract*
2. *permutatio stricte sic dicta* (exchange in the original sense)
   1. Exchange proper
   2. *mutuum* (*usurae*) [loan] (interest)
   3. *emptio venditio* (buying and selling)

II. Out of the assured contract
pignus (pledge)

III. Out of the charitable contract
2. *commodatum* (lending, or loan contract)
3. *depositum* (storing of goods)

But why should I continue to fill the pages with things which I myself have rejected? Trichotomic divisions pervade the whole; it was written with tiresome prolixity and it abused the Roman concepts most barbarously in order to force them into my system. On the other hand, I thereby acquired a love for a general view of the material, at least to a certain extent.

At the end of the part on private law, I saw the falsity of the whole, which in its basis borders on Kantianism, but which deviates entirely from it in its application; and again it became clear to me that without philosophy nothing can be mastered. Thus I could once more throw myself into its arms with clear conscience, and I proceeded to write a new metaphysical system, at the end of which I was again forced to admit its incorrectness, as well as those of my own previous efforts in this direction.

In doing this, I acquired the habit of making excerpts from all the books I read—such as Lessing's *Laokoon*,[4] Solger's *Erwin*,[5] Winckelmann's history of art,[6] Luden's German history[7]—and to jot down reflections on the side. At the same time, I translated Tacitus's

---

4. Gotthold Ephraim Lessing, *Laokoon: oder ueber die Grenzen der Mahlerey und Poesie* (Berlin, 1766).
5. Karl Wilhelm Ferdinand Solger, *Erwin. Vier Gespraeche ueber das Schoene und die Kunst* (Berlin, 1815).
6. Johann Winckelmann, *Geschichte der Kunst des Alterthums* (2 Parts; Dresden, 1764 and 1767).
7. Heinrich Luden, *Geschichte des teutschen Volkes* (12 vols.; Gotha, 1825–1837).

Germania and Ovid's *Libri Tristium*, and began on my own, that is, out of grammars, to study English and Italian, in which I have not yet accomplished anything; I also read Klein's criminal law and his *Annals*,[8] and all the latest works of literature, the latter on the side, however.

At the end of the semester, I again sought the dances of the Muses and the music of Satyrs; and even in the last notebook which I sent you, Idealism, you will find, plays a role through forced humor (*Scorpion und Felix*) and shines through in an inept and fantastic drama (*Oulanem*), until finally it changes entirely and moves on to mere art form, mostly without inspired objects or vibrant ideas.

And yet, these recent poems are the only ones in which, suddenly, as if by a stroke of magic—alas, the stroke was a shattering one at first—the realm of true poetry shone for me like a distant fairy palace and thus all my own creation dissolved into nothingness.

With these manifold activities during the first semester, it is small wonder that many nights were passed in wakefulness, many battles were fought, many a stimulus within and without had to be coped with, so that at the end I did not emerge very enriched; I had neglected nature, art, and the world around me, and I alienated many friends. My physical condition deteriorated, and a doctor recommended the countryside; and thus, for the first time, I traversed the whole spreading city to the Stralow gate. I did not then anticipate that my stay there would change me from a pale weakling into a physically robust man.

A curtain had fallen, my holy of holies had been torn to shreds, and new gods had to replace it.

From Idealism, which, incidentally, I had compared to and enriched with Kantianism and Fichteism, I moved to investigate the Idea in the reality itself. If the gods had formerly dwelt' above the earth, they now became its center.

I had read fragments of Hegel's philosophy,[9] the grotesque, rocklike melody of which did not appeal to me. Once again I wished to dive into the sea, but with the definite intention of finding our spiritual nature as essential, concrete, and solidly rounded as the physical one;

---

8. Ernst Ferdinand Klein, *Grundsaetze des gemeinen deutschen peinlichen Rechts nebst Bemerkung der preussischen Gesetze* (2d ed., Halle, 1799).

Annalen der Gesetzgebung und Rechtsgelehrsamkeit in den Preussischen Staaten (26 vols.; Berlin and Stettin, 1788–1809).

9. Georg Wilhelm Friedrich Hegel, *Phaenomologie des Geistes* in his *Werke*, Vol. 11 (Berlin, 1832).

Wissenschaft der Logik in his *Werke*, Vols. III–V (Berlin, 1833–34).

Vorlesungen ueber die Geschichte der Philosophie in his *Werke*, Vol. XIV (Berlin, 1833).

Encyclopaedie der philosophischen Wissenschaften im Grundrisse (3d ed., Heidelberg, 1830).

no longer would I practice the arts of fencing but hold the pure pearl up to the sunlight.

I wrote a dialogue of approximately twenty-four pages: "Cleanthes, or the Starting Point and Necessary Progress of Philosophy." It combined to a certain extent art and learning, which previously had been separated; and I plunged vigorously into the work itself, into a philosophical-dialectical development of the godhead as it manifests itself as the concept itself, as religion, as nature, as history. My last theme was the beginning of the Hegelian system; and this task, for which I was somewhat prepared by my reading of natural science, Schelling,[10] and history, has caused me endless headaches, being written in such a [words crossed out in manuscript]—(since it was meant actually to constitute a new system of logic), that I myself can scarcely follow it now. This beloved offspring of mine, tended in moonlight, lures me on treacherously, like a false siren, into the arms of the enemy.

I was so angry I was unable to think at all for a couple of days, ran around like a madman in the garden close to the dirty waters of the Spree, a river of which it has been said that it "washes souls and dilutes tea" [Heinrich Heine, *Die Nordsee*]; I even joined my landlord in a hunting party, then hastened back and felt like embracing every loafer at every street corner.

Shortly thereafter I pursued only positive studies; I read Savigny's *Property*,[11] Feuerbach's and Grolmann's criminal law,[12] Cramer's *De verborum significatione*,[13] Wening-Ingenheim's pandect system,[14] and Muehlenbruch's *Doctrina Pandectarum*,[15] the last of which I have not finished. I also studied some of Lauterbach's works,[16] civil law and in particular ecclesiastical law, including the first part of Gratian's *Concordia discordantium canonum*,[17] of which I have read virtually the

---

10. Friedrich Wilhelm Joseph Schelling, *Philosophische Schriften*, Vol. I (Landshut, 1809).

11. Friedrich Carl von Savigny, *Das Recht des Besitzes* (Giessen, 1803).

12. Johann Paul Anselm Feuerbach, *Revision der Grundsaetze und Grundbegriffe des positiven peinlichen Rechts* (2 Parts, Erfurt and Chemnitz, 1799–1800); *Lehrbuch des gemeinen in Deutschland gueltigen peinlichen Rechts* (4th ed., Giessen, 1808).
Karl von Grolmann, *Grundsaetze der Criminalrechts-Wissenschaft* (4th ed., Giessen, 1825).

13. Andreas Wilhelm Cramer, *De verborum significatione tituli pandectarum et codicis cum variae lectionis apparatu* (Kiel, 1811).

14. Johann Nepomuk Wening-Ingenheim, *Lehrbuch des Gemeinen Civilrechtes* (3 vols.; 4th ed., Munich, 1831–32).

15. Christian Friedrich Muehlenbruch, *Doctrina pandectarum. Halis Saxonum 1823 bis 1825* (3 vols., 3d ed., 1838).

16. Wolfgang Adam Lauterbach, *Collegium theorico-practicum. Ad L. Pandectarum Libros methodo synthetica* (43 vols., Tuebingen, 1690–1714).

17. In Gratian's *Corpus iuris canonici* (published in the twelfth century).

whole corpus, including the appendix, and made excerpts, and also Lancelotti's *Institutiones*.[18] Then I translated part of Aristotle's *Rhetoric*, read the famous Bacon's (Baron Verulam) *De augmentis scientiarum*,[19] occupied myself very much with Reimarus, whose book, *Von den Kunsttrieben der Tiere*,[20] I once had studied with great pleasure. I also took up German law, but here I restricted my reading to the capitularies of the Frankish kings and the popes' letters to them. From grief over Jenny's illness and my fruitless intellectual labors, from a consuming anger over having to make an idol of a viewpoint I hated, I fell sick, as I have already told you, dear Father. My health restored, I burned all my poems and sketches for short novels, etc., laboring under the illusion that I could abandon them altogether—of which there is as yet no evidence.

During my illness, I came to know Hegel's works, as well as most of his disciples, from beginning to end. As a result of several meetings with friends at Stralow, I got into a Doctors [of Philosophy] club, which had among its members university lecturers [*Privatdozenten*] and my most intimate Berlin friend, Dr. Rutenberg.[21] In the course of our discussion many an opposing opinion came to light and I clung ever more tightly to my own world outlook, of which, in truth, I had believed myself free, but any resounding ideas I might have had were muted; and so I was seized with a rage for irony, as so often happens when there is that much negativism. This was aggravated by Jenny's silence. I could not rest until I had grasped modernity and the point of view of modern scholarship by turning out a few poor productions, such as *Der Besuch* [The Visit], etc.

If perhaps I have failed to convey to you either a clear idea or all the details, as well as the nuances, of the past semester, do please forgive me, dear Father, on account of my eagerness to speak of the present.

Herr von Chamisso[22] sent me a measly note in which he says "he regrets that his Almanac cannot use my contributions, because it has long since gone to press." I swallowed his note in anger. Wigand,[23] the bookdealer, forwarded my plan to Dr. [Karl] Schmidt, publisher

---

18. Giovanni Paolo Lancelotti, *Institutiones iuris canonici* (in *Corpus iuris canonici*).

19. Francis Bacon, *De dignitate et augmentis scientiarum* (London, 1623).

20. Hermann Samuel Reimarus, *Allgemeine Betrachtungen ueber die Triebe der Thiere, hauptsaechlich ueber ihre Kunst-Triebe* (Hamburg, 1760).

21. Adolf Rutenberg (1808–1869), a Young Hegelian, was a German newspaperman and editor (of the *National-Zeitung* in 1848).

22. Adelbert von Chamisso (1781–1838), a French-born German poet, was the author of the famous *Peter Schlemihls wunderbare Geschichte* (1814).

23. Otto Wigand (1795–1877) was a Leipzig publisher and bookdealer.

of Wunder's Store of Good Cheese and Bad Literature.[24] I am enclosing Wigand's letter; Schmidt has not answered yet. In the meantime, I shall by no means give up this plan, all the more so as all the famous experts on aesthetics of the Hegelian school, through the good offices of Instructor [Bruno] Bauer, who plays a great role among them, as well as my coadjutor Dr. Rutenberg, have promised to cooperate.

In regard to the question of a government career, my dear Father, I have recently made the acquaintance of Assistant Judge [Assessor] Schmidthaenner, who advised me to enter it after passing the third law examination; this would appeal to me all the more since I really prefer jurisprudence to any study of public administration. The gentleman in question told me that from the Münster District Court in Westphalia he himself and many others made it to assistant judge in three years, which, he says, is not difficult to do—provided, of course, that one works hard—since there the stages [of promotion] are not as strictly fixed as they are in Berlin and other places. If, as assistant judge, one later attains the doctorate, there are much better prospects for immediate appointment as professor extraordinary, as happened in the case of Mr. Gaertner[25] in Bonn after he wrote a mediocre book on provincial codes of law, his only other title to fame being that he calls himself a member of the Hegelian school of law. However, my dear Father, best of fathers, would it not be possible for us to talk this over face to face? Eduard's [Karl's brother] condition, dear Mother's illness, your own indisposition, which I hope is not very serious, all makes me wish, indeed makes it virtually necessary, for me to hurry home. I would, indeed, have been there already, if I had not been in doubt about your permission, your consent.

Believe me, my dear, beloved Father, this is not a selfish wish (although I would be blissful to see Jenny again); I am, however, motivated by a thought which I may not put into words. In some respects it would be difficult for me to come, and yet, as my own sweet Jenny writes, such considerations must give way to the fulfillment of duties, which are sacred.

Whatever your decision, I implore you, dear Father, not to show this letter to Angel Mother [*Engelsmutter*], or at least not this page of it. My unexpected arrival may perhaps cheer up that great, splendid woman.

My letter to her was written long before the arrival of Jenny's dear letter, and thus, unwittingly, I may have written too much about matters that are not suitable or very little so.

---

24. Julius Wunder had a book business in Leipzig between 1833 and 1841.
25. Gustav Friedrich Gaertner (d. 1841) was a professor of law in Bonn.

In the hope that the clouds which hang over our family will gradually pass; that I may be permitted to share your sufferings and mingle my tears with yours, and in your presence perhaps demonstrate the deep affection, the boundless love, which I have often expressed poorly; in the hope that you too, dear, eternally beloved Father, mindful of the confused state of my storm-tossed soul, will forgive where the heart must often have seemed to err as my overburdened spirit stifled it; in the hope that you will soon be fully restored to health so that I shall be able to press you close to my heart and tell you all that I feel,

I remain your ever loving son, KARL.

Forgive, dear Father, the illegible handwriting and the bad style; it is nearly four o'clock; the candle has burned out completely, and my eyes are blurred; a deep restlessness has overwhelmed me; I shall not be able to mollify the specters that haunt me until I am in your dear presence.

Please greet for me my sweet, splendid Jenny. I have already read her letter twelve times, and every time I discover new charms in it. In every respect, even in style, it is the most beautiful letter I can imagine a woman writing.

The State as Educator

From the "Leading Article in No. 179 of the *Kölnische Zeitung*," in *Rheinische Zeitung*, July 12, 1842

. . . THE EDUCATION of our school youth is based as much on the old classics and general sciences as on the catechism.

According to Hermes,[1] the State differentiates itself from a kindergarten not by content but by size, it extends its "nursing" further.

But the "public" education of the State is rather the rational and public existence of the State. Only the State trains its members in that it makes them into political members; in that it transforms individual aims into public aims, raw drive into ethical tendency, natural independence into spiritual freedom; in that the individual enjoys his life in the life of the totality and the totality enjoys itself in the character of the individual.

But the leading article on the contrary makes the State not into a union of free men who mutually educate one another but into a heap of adults who are destined to be educated haughtily and to move from the "narrow" schoolroom into the "wider" schoolroom.

---

1. Carl Heinrich Hermes (1800–1856), an editor of the conservative *Kölnische Zeitung*.

Education and Pauperism

From "Critcial Marginal Notes on the Article 'The King of Prussia and Social Reform. By a Prussian,'" in *Vorwärts!* August 7 and 10, 1844[1]

THUS Dr. Kay[2] in his brochure, "Recent Measures for the Promotion of Education in England," for example, reduces everything to *neglected education*. Guess on what grounds! From lack of education the worker fails to comprehend the "natural laws of commerce," laws which *necessarily* reduce him to pauperism. Hence he resists. This can only "embarrass the prosperity of English manufacturers and English commerce, shake the mutual confidence of businessmen, and diminish the stability of political and social institutions."

So great is the brainlessness of the English bourgeoisie and its press concerning pauperism, this national epidemic of England! . . .

Thus far the "Prussian" has not proved anything peculiar in the procedure of the King of Prussia. But *why*, the great man exclaims with rare naiveté: "Why does not the King of Prussia immediately order the education of all destitute children?" Why does he first turn to the authorities and wait upon their plans and proposals?

The overclever "Prussian" will calm himself when he learns that the King of Prussia is no more original in this respect than he has been in other actions, that in fact he has taken the only course a chief of state *can* take.

Napoleon wanted to destroy beggary at one stroke. He ordered his officials to prepare plans for the eradication of beggary throughout France. The project kept him waiting; he lost patience and wrote to

---

1. Text in *Karl Marx on Revolution*, Vol. I of The Karl Marx Library, p. 10.
2. James Phillips Kay-Shuttleworth (1804–1877), a Manchester physician.

his Minister of the Interior, Crétet, commanding him to destroy beggary within one month, saying; "One should not depart from this world without leaving traces that commend our memory to posterity. Do not make me wait another three or four months for a report. You have young lawyers, clever prefects, well-trained engineers of bridges and roads; put them all to work, and do not fall asleep in the routine office work."

In a few months everything was done. On July 5, 1808, a decree suppressing beggary was issued. How? By means of *dépôts*, which were so quickly transformed into penal establishments that soon the poor could be admitted to them only by way of the police court. And despite that, M. Noailles du Gard, member of the legislative corps, exclaimed, "Eternal gratitude to the hero who secures for the needy a place of refuge and for the poor a means of life. Childhood will no longer be neglected, poor families will no longer be deprived of resources, nor workers of encouragement and employment. Our progress shall no longer be retarded by the disgusting spectacle of infirmities and shameful poverty."

The last cynical passage is the only truth in this eulogy.

If Napoleon seeks the views of his officers of justice, prefects, and engineers, why shouldn't the King of Prussia do the same with his officials?

Why did not Napoleon *immediately* order the abolition of beggary? Of equal value is the "Prussian" question: "Why does not the King of Prussia immediately order the education of destitute children?" Does the "Prussian" know what the King must decree? Nothing less than the *abolition of the proletariat*. To educate children, one must feed them and free them from paid labor. The feeding and educating of destitute children—that is, the feeding and educating of the entire growing proletariat—would be the abolition of the proletariat and of pauperism.

Circumstances Change Education

From "Theses on Feuerbach," written in spring 1845, Section 3.

THE MATERIALIST DOCTRINE that men are the products of circumstances and education, hence changed men are the products of different circumstances and changed education, forgets that these circumstances are changed by men and that the educator himself must be educated. Necessarily, therefore, it divides society into two parts, of which one is superior to society (for example, Robert Owen).

The coincidence of the changing of circumstances and of human activity can be understood rationally only as *revolutionary practice*.

Education and Environment

From Marx and Engels, *The Holy Family* (1845), Chapter IV.

CONDILLAC, Locke's immediate follower and French translator, at once opposed Locke's sensualism in favor of seventeenth-century metaphysics. . . .

In his *Essai sur l'Origine des Connaissances Humaines* [Amsterdam, 1746] he consummated Locke's ideas and proved that not only the soul but also the senses, not only the art of creating ideas but also the art of sensuous perception, are matters of *experience* and *habit*. Hence the whole development of man depends on *education* and *environment*. It was only by the *eclectic* philosophy that Condillac was supplanted in the French schools.

The difference between French and English materialism is the same as the difference between the two nations. The French endowed English materialism with wit, flesh, blood, and eloquence. They imparted to it the temperament and grace it had lacked. They *civilized* it.

In Helvétius, who likewise derives from Locke, materialism receives its proper French character. He conceived it primarily in connection with social life (Helvétius, *De l'Homme, de ses Facultés intellectuels et de son Éducation* [London, 1775]). Sensuous qualities and self-love, enjoyment of understood personal interest, are the basis of all morality. The natural equality of human intelligence, the unity of the progress of reason and the progress of industry, the natural goodness of man, and the omnipotence of education are main factors of his system. . . .

It requires no great acuteness to see from the teachings of materialism on such matters as the original goodness and equal intellectual endowment of men, the omnipotence of experience, habit, education, and the influence of environment on man, the great importance of industry, the justification of enjoyment, etc., that there is a necessary connection between materialism and communism and socialism. If man derives all knowledge, sensation, etc., from the world of the senses and sense experience, it follows that the empirical world must be so constructed that in it he experiences the truly human and becomes aware of himself as man. If properly understood interest is the principle of all morality, it follows that the private interests of men coincide with the interest of humanity. If man is unfree in the material sense, that is, free, not through the negative power of avoiding this or that, but through the positive power of asserting his true individuality, it follows that crime must not be punished in the individual but that antisocial sources of crime must be destroyed and each man given the social scope for his essential life-expression. If man is shaped by circumstances, his circumstances must be made human. If man is by nature social, he will develop his true nature only in society, and the power of his nature must be measured not by the power of separate individuals but by the power of society.

The Educated and the Uneducated

From Marx and Engels, *The German Ideology* (1845–46),
Chapter III, D ("Hierarchy")

ONE MORE EXAMPLE of the domination of the Idea in everyday life.
Since schoolmasters may be consoled for the scantiness of their pay by
the holiness of the cause they serve (which can happen only in Germany), Jacques le bonhomme actually believes that this phraseology
is the reason for their low salary (p. 100). He believes that "the Holy"
in the present-day bourgeois world has a real money value, he believes
that the paltry resources of the Prussian state (see Browning,[1] among
others) would be so increased by the abolition of "the Holy" that every
village schoolmaster could be suddenly paid a salary like a Minister.

This is the hierarchy of nonsense.

The "cornerstone of the magnificent cathedral" of hierarchy, as the
great Michelet[2] says, is "sometimes" the work of "One." "One sometimes divides people into two classes, the educated and the uneducated."
One sometimes divides apes into two classes, the tailed and the tailless.
"The first, insofar as they were worthy of their name, occupied themselves with thoughts, with the spirit." They "dominated in the post-
Christian era and for their thoughts they demanded—respect." The
uneducated (the animal, the child, the Negro) are "powerless"
against thoughts and "are dominated by them. This is the meaning of
hierarchy."

The "heducated" (the youth, the Mongol, the Modern) are,

---

1. G. Browning, *The Domestic and Financial Condition of Great Britain*
(London, 1834).

2. Carl Ludwig Michelet, *Geschichte der letzten Systeme der Philosophie in
Deutschland von Kant bis Hegel* [History of the Latest System of Philosophy in
Germany from Kant to Hegel] (2 vols., Berlin, 1837–38).

therefore, again occupied with "*the* spirit," the pure thought, etc.; they are metaphysicians by profession and, in the last analysis, Hegelians. "Hence" the "unheducated" are the non-Hegelians. Hegel was without doubt the most "heducated" Hegelian and therefore in his case it must "become apparent what a longing the most educated has for things." Specifically, the "heducated" and the "unheducated" are within themselves in conflict with one another; indeed, in every man the "heducated" and "unheducated" are in conflict. And since, in Hegel, the greatest longing for things, i.e., which becomes apparent in the "unheducated," it also becomes apparent here that the "most heducated" is at the same time the "most unheducated."

The education law shows us the alliance of the young Catholics, with the old Voltaireans. Could the rule of the united bourgeoisie be anything else but the coalesced despotism of the pro-Jesuit Restoration and the make-believe freethinking July Monarchy? Had not the weapons that the one bourgeois faction had distributed among the people against the other faction, in their mutual struggle for supremacy, again been torn from it, the people, since the latter was confronting their united dictatorship? Nothing has aroused the Paris shopkeeper more than its coquettish *étalage* [display] of Jesuitism, not even the rejection of the *concordats à l'amiable*.[2]

. . . Unhindered by the provocations of the government, which only heightened the general exasperation over the existing situation, the election committee, wholly under the influence of the workers, put forward three candidates for Paris: Deflotte, Vidal, and Carnot. Deflotte was a June deportee, amnestied through one of Bonaparte's popularity-seeking ideas; he was a friend of Blanqui and had taken part in the attempt of May 15.[3] Vidal, known as a communist writer through his book *Concerning the Distribution of Wealth*,[4] was formerly secretary to Louis Blanc in the Luxembourg Commission. Carnot, son of the man of the Convention who had organized the victory, the least compromised member of the National party, Minister of Education in the Provisional Government and the Executive Commission, was through his democratic public education bill a living protest against the education law of the Jesuits. . . .[5]

---

2. A law providing for a delay in paying debts at lower interest rates.
3. On May 15, 1848, Paris workers attempted to overthrow the French provisional government and were defeated.
4. François Vidal, *De la Repartition des Richesses* . . . (Paris, 1846).
5. Text in *Karl Marx on Revolution*, Vol. I of The Karl Marx Library, p. 227.

Charitable English Schools

From "Achievements of the Ministry,"* in *New-York Daily Tribune,*
April 27, 1853

. . . WHEN LORD JOHN RUSSELL first announced the program of the
Coalition Ministry, and when it was received amid general conster-
nation, his adherents exclaimed, "We must have something to be en-
thusiastic at. Public education shall be the thing. Our Russell is
breeding a wonderful Education scheme. You will hear of it."

Now we have heard of it. It was on the 4th of April that Russell
gave a general description of his intended Educational Reform. Its
principal features consist in enabling the municipal councils to levy a
local rate for the assistance of *existing* schools in which the Church of
England doctrines are required to be taught. As to the Universities,
those pet-children of the State Church, those chief opponents of every
reform, Lord John hopes "that the Universities will reform themselves."
The malversation of the charities destined for educational establishments is notorious. Their value may be guessed from the following:
"There are 24 of £2,000 a year and under £3,000, 10 of £3,000 and
under £4,000, 4 of £4,000 and under £5,000, 2 of £5,000 and under
£6,000, 3 of £8,000 and under £9,000, and single ones of £10,000,
£15,000, £20,000, £29,000, £30,000 and £35,000 a year each." It
needs no great capacity to conceive why the oligarchs living on the
malversation of these funds are very cautious in dealing with them.
Russell proposes: "Charities are to be examined into, those under £30
per annum in the County Courts, those above by the Master of the
Rolls. But *no suit* in either of those Courts is to be instigated *without
the permission of a Committee of the Council appointed for the pur-*

---

* By Marx and Engels.

pose." The *permission* of a committee is necessary to institute a suit in the Imperial Courts to redress the plunder of the charities originally destined for the education of the people. A permission! But Russell, even with this reservation, feels not quite sure. He adds: "If the administration of a school is *found* to be corrupt, *nobody but the Committee of Council shall be allowed to interfere.*"

This is a true reform in the old English sense of the word. It neither creates anything new nor abolishes anything old. It aims at conserving the old system by giving it a more reasonable form and teaching it, so to say, new manners. This is the mystery of the "hereditary wisdom" of English oligarchical legislation. It simply consists in making abuses hereditary by refreshing them, as it were, from time to time, by infusion of new blood.

If everybody must confess that the Jewish Disabilities Bill was a *little* attempt at establishing religious tolerance, the Canada Reserves Bill a *little* attempt at granting Colonial Self-Government, the Education Bill a *little* attempt at avoiding public education, Gladstone's financial scheme is, undoubtedly, a *mighty little* attempt at dealing with that giant monster, the National Debt of Great Britain.

Educational Qualifications

From "The New British Reform Bill," in *New-York Daily Tribune*, March 17, 1859

PASSING NOW from the countries to the boroughs, we arrive at the new fancy franchises that are partly derived from Lord John Russell's abortive schemes of 1852 and 1854, and are partly due to the genius which hatched the convoluted perplexities of Lord Ellenborough's unhappy India bill. There are, first, some so-called educational qualifications, which, as Mr. Disraeli ironically remarked, independent as they are of scientific acquirements betoken the education of the classes they concern, "to have involved some considerable investment," and may therefore be considered to belong to the general category of property qualifications. The right of vote is consequently to be conferred upon graduates, the clergy of the Church of England, ministers of all other denominations, barristers, pleaders and conveyancers, solicitors and proctors, medical men, certified schoolmasters; in a word, on the members of the different liberal professions, or, as the French used to call it in M. Guizot's time, on the "capacities."

German Student Duelling

From "The War in Europe . . ." in *New-York Daily Tribune*,
May 9, 1859

IN GERMAN UNIVERSITIES, after the students have been dislodged, at about 11 o'clock at night, by the academical authorities, from their various beer-houses, the several societies among the fraternity generally assemble on the market-place, if the weather is propitious. There the members of each society or "color" begin a game of "chaff" with those of any other color—the aim of which is to produce one of those frequent and not very dangerous duels which compose one of the chief features of student life. In these preliminary controversies on the market-place, the great art consists in so wording your hits that no actual or formal insult is contained in them, although as much as possible you vex your opponent, and at last make him lose his temper, so that he comes out with that conventional, formal insult which compels you to send him a challenge.

Compulsory Education

Minutes of the General Council,* August 10, 1869

[*The education question came then on for discussion. Citizen* Eccarius
*read so much of the Geneva Resolutions as referred to training and
education of children and adolescents*[1] *and proposed that it be adhered
to. . . .*]

CITIZEN MARX said there was a peculiar difficulty connected with this
question. On the one hand, a change of social circumstances was required to establish a proper system of education; on the other hand,
a proper system of education was required to bring about a change of
social circumstances, we must therefore commence where we were.

The question treated at the Congress was whether education was
to be national or private.[2] National education had been looked upon
as governmental, but that was not necessarily the case. In Massachusetts every township was bound to provide schools for primary education for all the children. In towns of more than 5,000 inhabitants higher

---

* Written in English.
1. Resolutions of the First Congress Assembled at Geneva, September 1866:
"By education we understand three things. Firstly: Mental education. Secondly:
Bodily education, such as is given in schools, by gymnastics, and by military
exercise. Thirdly: Technological training, which imparts the general principles of
all process of production, and, simultaneously initiates the child and young person
in the practical use and handling of the elementary instruments of all trades. A
gradual and progressive course of mental, gymnastic, and technological training
ought to correspond with the classification of the juvenile laborers. The costs of
the technological schools ought to be partly met by the sale of their products.
The combination of paid productive labor, mental education, bodily exercise,
and polytechnic training will raise the working class far above the level of the
higher and middle classes."
2. General education was discussed also at the Congresses of Geneva (1866),
Lausanne (1867), and Brussels (1868).

schools for technical education had to be provided, in larger towns still higher. The state contributed something but not much. In Massachusetts one-eighth of the local taxes went for education, in New York one-fifth. The school committees which administered the schools were local, they appointed the schoolmasters and selected the books. The fault of the American system was that it was too much localized, the education given depended upon the state of culture prevailing in each district. There was a cry for a central supervision. The taxation for schools was compulsory, but the attendance of children was not. Property had to pay the taxes and the people who paid the taxes wanted that the money was usefully applied. Education might be national without being governmental. Government might appoint inspectors whose duty it was to see that the laws were obeyed, just as the factory inspectors looked after the observance of the factory acts, without any power of interfering with the course of education itself.

The Congress might without hesitation adopt that education was to be compulsory. As to children being prevented from working, one thing was certain: it would not reduce wages and people would get used to it.

The Proudhonists maintained that gratuitous education was nonsense, because the state had to pay for it; of course somebody had to pay, but not those who could least afford it. [Marx] was not in favor of gratuitous college education.

As Prussian education had been talked so much of, he would conclude by observing that the Prussian system was only calculated to make good soldiers.

Technological Education

Karl Marx, Remarks (in English) at the meeting of the General Council of the International, August 17, 1869[1]

CITIZEN MARX said: upon certain points we were unanimous.

The discussion had started with the proposition to reaffirm the Geneva [International's Congress] resolution which demanded that mental education should be combined with bodily labor, with gymnastics and technological training; nothing had been said against that.

The technological training advocated by proletarian writers was meant to compensate for the deficiencies occasioned by the division of labor which prevented apprentices from acquiring a thorough knowledge of their business. This had been taken hold of and misconstrued into what the middle class understood by technical education.

As to Mrs. Law's[2] Church budget it would be good policy for the Congress to declare against the Church.

Citizen Milner's proposition[3] was not suitable to be introduced in connection with the schools; it was a kind of education that the young must get from the adults in the everyday struggle of life. He could not accept Warren[4] as a bible, it was a question upon which few could

---

1. The Minutes of the meeting were written by the Secretary, J. George Eccarius.

2. Harriet Law (1832–1897), an English member of the International who advocated atheism; at the above meeting she said: "The property of the Church must be secularized and devoted to schools."

3. At the August 10th meeting, George Milner, an Irish member of the General Council, remarked: ". . . In any scheme of education the consent of all classes was required, but the working class ought to insist that with production the children ought to learn the laws that regulate the value of the produce of their labor."

4. Josiah Warren (ca. 1798–1874), an American philosophical anarchist and follower of Robert Owen.

agree. We might add that such education cannot be given at school, but must be given by adults.

Nothing could be introduced either in primary or higher schools that admitted of party and class interpretation. Only subjects such as the physical sciences, grammar, etc., were fit matter for schools. The rules of grammar, for instance, could not differ, whether explained by a religious Tory or a freethinker. Subjects that admitted of different conclusions must be excluded and left for the adults to such teachers as Mrs. Law, who gave instruction in religion.[5]

---

5. In *The Bee-Hive* of August 21, 1869, this passage of Marx's comments was reported as follows: "As to political economy, religion, and other questions, they could not be admitted into the primary, nor even the higher schools, that was a kind of education which must rest with the adult, and must be left to the lecture room, to such schoolmasters as Mrs. Law."

Education Under the Commune (I)

From first draft of *The Civil War in France*, written April–May 1871

OF COURSE the Commune had no sufficient time to reorganize public education; but by the elimination of religious and clerical elements it undertook to emancipate the people intellectually. It appointed (on April 28) a committee for the organization of general (elementary) as well as professional education. It decreed that all educational supplies such as books, maps, paper, etc., be distributed by the teachers free of charge, they themselves receiving them from the appropriate *mairies*. No teacher is entitled, for no matter what reason, to demand payment for these educational supplies. . . .

It senses that only the working class can emancipate it from the rule of the parsons, that science can be transformed from a tool of class rule into a power of the people, that men of science can be changed from panderers of class prejudice, job-hunting political parasites, and confederates of capital into free representatives of the intellect. Science can play its real role only in the Republic of Labor. . . .

(II)

From *The Civil War in France* (1871), Section III*

HAVING ONCE got rid of the standing army and the police, the physical-force elements of the old government, the Commune was anxious to break the spiritual force of repression, the "parson power," by the disestablishment and disendowment of all churches as proprietary bodies. The priests were sent back to the recesses of private life, there to feed upon the alms of the faithful in imitation of their predecessors, the Apostles. The whole of the educational institutions were opened to the people gratuitously, and at the same time cleared of all interference of church and state. Thus not only was education made accessible to all, but science itself freed from the fetters which class prejudice and governmental force had imposed upon it.

* Text in *Karl Marx on Revolution,* Vol. I of The Karl Marx Library, p. 350.

Students in Russia

From Marx and Engels (with the assistance of Paul Lafargue), *A Plot Against the International Working Men's Association*, written in French and published as a brochure in 1873; this translation, by the editor of this volume, is from a German version by S. Kokosky, published in 1874.*

In 1861, in reaction to the fiscal measures which aimed to keep poor young people out of institutions of higher learning, as well as to the disciplinary regulations which tended to submit them to the discretionary rule of police agents, the students unanimously rose in protests which spread into street meetings and grew into huge demonstrations. The Petersburg University was closed for a time and the students were thrown into prison or banished. These actions of the government drove the youth into secret societies, which, of course, had the fateful result that a large part of their membership went to prison, into exile, or ended in Siberia. Others set up funds for mutual support, to enable poor students to continue their studies. The most serious among them were determined not to give the government any pretext for the suppression of these funds, which were organized in such a way that they were managed in small circles. At the same time these circles provided an opportunity for discussing political and social questions. Socialist ideas had already penetrated so far among the higher Russian school youths (the great majority of them sons of peasants and other poor people) that they immediately thought of a practical application of these ideas. In the schools, this movement, whose theoretical soul was Chernyshevski (now in Siberia), became more and more general, and

* For a substantial portion of the text, see *Karl Marx on the First International*, Vol. III of The Karl Marx Library, pp. 251–66.

threw into Russian society a propertyless youth, which had come out of the lower classes and was educated in and permeated by socialist ideas. . . .

In March 1861 the youth in Russian universities spoke out energetically for the liberation of Poland; in fall 1861 the students attempted to resist the government coup which aimed, by means of disciplinary and fiscal measures, to rob the poor students (more than two-thirds of the total) of the possibility of participating in higher education. The government treated their protests as riots; in Petersburg, Moscow, and Kazan hundreds of young people were thrown into prison, driven from the universities, or expelled after a three-months' prison term. And out of fear that these young people would aggravate the dissatisfaction of the peasants, a decree of the State Council forbade former students all access to public offices in the countryside. The persecutions did not stop there. Professors like Pavlov[1] were banished; public lectures organized by students expelled from the universities were closed; new persecutions began under the slightest pretexts; the barely authorized "Cash of the Student Youth" was suddenly suppressed; newspapers were suspended. All this moved the radical party to the greatest indignation and excitement and forced it to take refuge in a secret press. The manifesto of this party appeared under the title, "Young Russia,"[2] with a motto from the writings of [Robert] Owen. This manifesto gave a clear and distinct picture of the internal conditions of the country, the position of the various parties and of the press, and concluded thereby, while it proclaimed communism, the necessity for a social revolution. It called upon all able persons to rally to the radical flag. . . .

---

1. In 1862, the Russian historian Platon Vassilyevich Pavlov was banished from St. Petersburg for his activities in behalf of revolutionary students.
2. The revolutionary Proclamation, *Molodaya Rossyia* (Young Russia), was issued in May 1862.

Universal Free Education

From "Marginal Notes to the Program of the German Workers' Party"
(Gotha Program) (1875*), Part IV

B. "The German Workers' party demands as the intellectual and ethical basis of the state:

"1. Universal and equal elementary education by the state. Universal compulsory school attendance. Free instruction."

"Equal elementary education"? What idea lies behind these words? Is it believed that in present-day society (and it is only with this one has to deal) education can be *equal* for all classes? Or is it demanded that the upper classes also shall be compulsorily reduced to the modicum of education—the elementary school—that alone is compatible with the economic conditions not only of the wage workers but of the peasants as well?

"Universal compulsory school attendance. Free instruction." The former exists even in Germany, the second in Switzerland and in the United States in the case of elementary schools. If in some states of the latter country higher educational institutions are also "free," that only means in fact defraying the cost of the education of the upper classes from the general tax receipts. Incidentally, the same holds good for "free administration of justice" demanded under A, 5. The administration of criminal justice is to be had free everywhere; that of civil justice is concerned almost exclusively with conflicts over property and hence affects almost exclusively the possessing classes. Are they to carry on their litigation at the expense of the national coffers?

The paragraph on the schools should at least have demanded tech-

---

* Text in *Karl Marx on Revolution*, Vol. I of The Karl Marx Library, pp. 504-5.

nical schools (theoretical and practical) in combination with the elementary school.

"Elementary education by the state" is altogether objectionable. Defining by a general law the expenditures on the elementary schools, the qualifications of the teaching staff, the branches of instruction, etc., and, as is done in the United States, supervising the fulfillment of these legal specifications by state inspectors, is a very different thing from appointing the state as the educator of the people! Government and church should rather be equally excluded from any influence on the school. Particularly, indeed, in the Prusso-German Empire (and one should not take refuge in the rotten subterfuge that one is speaking of a "state of the future"; we have seen how matters stand in this respect) the state has need, on the contrary, of a very stern education by the people.

But the whole program, for all its democratic clang, is tainted through and through by the Lassallean sect's servile belief in the state, or, what is no better, by a democratic belief in miracles, or rather it is a compromise between these two kinds of belief in miracles, both equally remote from socialism.

"Freedom of science" says a paragraph of the Prussian Constitution. Why, then, here?

"Freedom of conscience"! If one desired at this time of the *Kulturkampf*[1] to remind liberalism of its old catchwords, it surely could have been done only in the following form: Everyone should be able to attend to his religious as well as his bodily needs without the police sticking their noses in. But the Workers' party ought at any rate in this connection to have expressed its awareness of the fact that bourgeois "freedom of conscience" is nothing but the toleration of all possible kinds of religious freedom of conscience, and that for its part it endeavors rather to liberate the conscience from the witchery of religion. But one chooses not to transgress the "bourgeois" level.

---

1. Cultural struggle; the reference is to Bismarck's struggle with the Catholic Church in Germany.

Education and the Commercial Worker

Excerpt from *Capital*, Vol. III (1894), Part IV, Chapter XVII

THE COMMERCIAL WORKER produces no surplus value directly. But the price of his labor is determined by the value of his labor power, hence by its costs of production, while the application of this labor power, its exertion, expenditure of energy, and wear and tear, is as in the case of every other wage laborer by no means limited by its value. His wage, therefore, is not necessarily proportionate to the mass of profit which he helps the capitalist to realize. What he costs the capitalist and what he brings in for him are two different things. He creates no direct surplus value, but adds to the capitalist's income by helping him to reduce the cost of realizing surplus value, inasmuch as he performs partly unpaid labor. The commercial worker, in the strict sense of the term, belongs to the better-paid class of wage workers—to those whose labor is classed as skilled and stands above average labor. Yet the wage tends to fall, even in relation to average labor, with the advance of the capitalist mode of production. This is due partly to the division of labor in the office, implying a one-sided development of the labor capacity, the cost of which does not fall entirely on the capitalist, since the laborer's skill develops by itself through the exercise of his function, and all the more rapidly as the division of labor makes it more one-sided. Secondly, because the preparatory training, knowledge of commercial practices, languages, etc., is more and more rapidly, easily, universally, and cheaply reproduced with the progress of science and public education, the more the capitalist mode of production directs teaching methods, etc., toward practical purposes. The universality of public education enables capitalists to recruit such laborers from classes that formerly had no access to such trades and were accustomed to a lower standard of living. Moreover, this increases supply, and hence competition. With a few exceptions, the labor power of these people is therefore devaluated with the progress of capitalist production. Their wage falls, while their labor capacity increases. The capitalist increases the number of these laborers whenever he has more value and profits to realize. The increase of this labor is always an effect, never a cause, of more surplus value.

WOMEN
AND CHILDREN

Child Psychology

Excerpts from Karl Marx, *"Debatten über Pressefreiheit und Publika-
tion der Landständischen Verhandlungen,"* in *Rheinische Zeitung,*
May 5, 1842

... IT IS WELL KNOWN that the first theoretical activity of the mind,
oscillating halfway between sensateness and thinking, is *counting*.
Counting is the child's first free theoretical act of reason. . . .

Space is the first thing the size of which impresses the child. It is
the size of the world that the child first experiences. Hence it considers
a grown man to be a great man. . . .

But the theoretical thinking of a child is quantitative: hence its
judgment and its practical thought is practical-sensate. The sensate
quality is the first tie that connects it with the world. The practical
sense, preferably the nose and mouth, are the first organs with which it
judges the world. . . .

The child, of course, stops with its sensate perception; it sees only
the particular. For the child, the invisible nerve threads that connect the
particular with the general . . . do not exist. The child believes the sun
revolves around the earth; the general revolves around the particular.
Hence the child does not believe in the *spirit* [*Geist*] but in *spirits*. . . .

Sex and Marriage

From the chapter on Marriage, in "The Philosophical Manifesto of the Historical School of Law," written in early August 1842*

"IN A PHILOSOPHICAL TREATMENT of positive law, marriage has been often regarded as more essential and rational than it would appear in an unsystematic investigation."

Gratification of the sex drive in marriage is, to be sure, suitable for Herr Hugo.[1] He even deduces a salutary moral from this fact:

"From this, as from numerous other relationships, one should have seen that it is not always unethical to treat the human body as a means to an end, and how this expression has been misunderstood even by Kant himself."

But the sanctification of the sex drive through exclusiveness, the restraint of the drive through law, ethical beauty which idealizes nature's command into a moment of spiritual union—the *spiritual essence* of marriage—all this is precisely what, for Herr Hugo, is dubious about marriage. But before we pursue further his frivolous shamelessness, let us for a moment hear a French philosopher as opposed to an historical German:

"In renouncing, for one man, that mysterious reserve whose divine law is imprinted in her heart, woman dedicates herself to that man for whom she suspends, in momentary abandon, that modesty which never leaves her; for him alone does she discard the veils which are in other respects her sanctuary and her ornament. From this stems the intimate

---

* This "Chapter," which was to appear as part of the larger article in the *Rheinische Zeitung* of August 9, 1842, was forbidden by the censorship.

1. Gustav Hugo (1764–1844) was a professor of law at Göttingen. The quotations in this article are from Hugo's *Lehrbuch eines civilistischen Cursus* (4th ed., 1819).

trust in her husband, the result of an exclusive relationship which can exist only between her and him, without her feeling tarnished; from this stems the husband's appreciation for a sacrifice and a mixture of desire and respect for one who, in sharing his pleasures, only seems to submit to him; from this stems everything that is *orderly* in the *social order*."

Thus the liberal French philosopher, *Benjamin Constant!*[2] And now let us hear the servile historical German:

"Much more doubtful is another proposition, namely that outside of marriage the gratification of the sex drive is *not* permissible! Our animal nature is opposed to this restriction. Our rational nature is even more so, because——" guess what!—"because a person would have to be virtually omniscient, because it would be challenging God to foresee the consequence of committing himself to one particular person for the gratification of one of the most powerful drives of nature!" "The feeling for beauty, free by its very nature, should be restrained, and what depends on it should be completely separated from it."

You can see what school our Young Germans[3] attended!

"This arrangement conflicts with our civic nature in that . . . finally the police undertake an almost insoluble task."

Clumsy philosophy, this, not to pay the same attention to the police themselves!

"Everything provided for in the detailed provision of the marriage law teaches us that marriage, no matter what principles one may apply to it, remains a very imperfect arrangement."

"But this confining of the sex drive to marriage, also has its important advantages—in that thereby the usual infectious diseases are avoided. Marriage spares the government quite a lot of difficulties. Finally, there is the consideration, so important everywhere, that what is a matter of private law is already something uniquely common." "Fichte says: The unmarried person is half a person. But I am very sorry [says Hugo] to have to declare that such a beautiful dictum, which puts even me above Christ, Fénelon, Kant, and Hume, is a gross exaggeration."

"As far as monogamy and polygamy are concerned, the subject obviously depends on the animal nature of man!"

---

2. Benjamin Constant (1767–1830), a French writer.
3. The Young Germans were a group of liberal writers under the influence of Heinrich Heine and Ludwig Börne.

The Divorce Law Draft

"The Divorce Law Draft" in *Rheinische Zeitung*, December 19, 1842

Cologne, December 18.

IN CONNECTION with the proposed divorce law,[1] the *Rheinische Zeitung* has taken a completely isolated position, the untenability of which has hitherto not been proven by any one. The *Rheinische Zeitung* agrees with the bill, insofar as it finds the existing Prussian marriage law unethical, the numerous and frivolous grounds for divorce inadmissible, and the existing proceedings not commensurate with the dignity of the matter—criticism that is applicable to the Old-Prussian court proceedings altogether. On the other hand, the *Rheinische Zeitung* raises the following main objections to the new bill: (1) that it substitutes mere revision for reform, since the Prussian statute law has been retained as fundamental, giving rise to considerable awkwardness and uncertainty; (2) that marriage is treated by the legislature, not as an ethical but as a religious and ecclesiastical institution, and thus the secular nature of marriage has not been recognized; (3) that the legal proceedings are very deficient and consist of an external composition of contradictory elements; (4) that, on the one hand, there is police severity contradicting the concept of marriage, and, on the other hand, there is too much indulgence toward so-called grounds of equity; (5) that the whole conception of the bill leaves much to be desired in logical consistency, precision, clarity, and thoroughness.

---

1. On October 20, 1842, the *Rheinische Zeitung* published the draft of a proposed divorce law, secretly prepared under the direction of Marx's University of Berlin professor, Friedrich Karl von Savigny. The publication of the draft led to wide discussion, and to the suppression of the *Rheinische Zeitung*, of which Marx was the editor.

Insofar as the opponents of the bill point to these deficiencies, we agree with them, but we can in no way approve their unconditional apology for the former system. We repeat again the statement we made earlier: "If the legislature cannot decree morality, it can even less recognize immorality as legal."[2] When we ask for the basis of the argument of these opponents (who are not opponents of the ecclesiastical view and of the other deficiencies mentioned), they always talk about the unhappiness of spouses bound to each other against their will. They take a eudaemonical position; they think of only two individuals, and forget the family; they forget that nearly every divorce is a separation of a family, and, even from a purely legal viewpoint, children and their property ought not to be dependent on arbitrary whims. If marriage were not the basis of the family, it would be no more the subject of legislation than is friendship. Those opponents, therefore, consider only the individual will, or rather the caprice of the spouses, but they do not consider the will of the marriage, the ethical substance of this relationship. The legislator, however, must regard himself as a naturalist. He does not make the laws; he does not invent them; he only formulates them; he expresses the inner laws of spiritual relationships in conscious, positive laws. If one must reproach the legislator with the grossest arbitrariness when he replaces the essence of the matter with his personal whims, so also he himself has no less the right to reproach private persons with the grossest arbitrariness when they wish to substitute their own caprices for the essence of the matter. Nobody is forced to enter into a marriage, but everybody must be forced to obey the laws of marriage once he enters into it. A person entering marriage does not make or invent it, any more than a swimmer invents nature and the laws of water and gravity. Marriage, therefore, cannot accommodate itself to his arbitrariness, but his arbitrariness must accommodate itself to marriage. He who breaks a marriage arbitrarily maintains that arbitrariness and lawlessness are the laws of marriage, for no reasonable person would have the presumptuousness to consider his acts to be privileged acts, acts appropriate to him alone; rather, he will pass them off as legal acts appropriate to all. What, then, do you oppose? Legislation by arbitrariness. But you surely will not want to make arbitrariness into law at the moment you accuse the legislator of arbitrariness.

Hegel says: "In itself, in accordance with its concept, marriage is indissoluble, but *only* in itself; that is, only in accordance with its concept."[3] This says nothing that is intrinsic to marriage. All ethical

---

2. "The Draft of the New Marriage Law," in supplement to *Rheinische Zeitung*, November 15, 1842.

3. Hegel, *Grundlinien der Philosophie des Rechts*, Appendix 163.

relationships are by their concepts indissoluble, as one can easily be convinced by assuming their truth. A true State, a true marriage, a true friendship—these are indissoluble; but no State, no marriage, no friendship corresponds completely to its concept; and, like actual friendship, even in the family, and like the actual State in world history, so actual marriage in the State is dissoluble. No ethical existence corresponds to its essence, or at least does not have to correspond to it. In nature itself there is dissolution and death, where a Being no longer fully corresponds to its destiny. Just as world history decides whether a State is so much at variance with the idea of the State that it no longer deserves to continue, so does the State decide under what conditions an existing marriage has ceased to be a marriage. Divorce is nothing but the declaration that the marriage is dead and that its existence is only pretense and deception. It is obvious that neither the arbitrariness of the legislator nor that of the private person but only the essence of the matter can decide whether or not a marriage is dead, for a death certificate, as is well known, depends on the facts of the case and not on the wishes of the interested parties. But if, in connection with physical death, you demand significant and undeniable proof, should not also the legislator have to substantiate, by indubitable symptoms, an ethical death, since to preserve the life of ethical relationships is not only his right but also his duty, the duty of its self-preservation?

The *certainty* that the conditions of ethical relationships no longer correspond to their existence, as objectively substantiated by science and general insight, will, of course, be present only when law is the conscious expression of the people's will formulated with their knowledge and consent. Let us add a word about making divorce easier or more difficult: Do you consider a natural body healthy, sound, and truly organized if any external shock, any injury, would destroy it? Would you not feel offended if it were established as an axiom that your friendship could not withstand the smallest accidents and must dissolve at any vagary? But in regard to marriage, the legislator can only determine when it *may* be dissolved, although it is already dissolved in its essence. The judicial dissolution can be only the recording of the inner dissolution. The viewpoint of the legislator is the viewpoint of necessity. Thus, the legislator honors marriage, recognizes its ethical essence, when he considers it strong enough to survive many conflicts without injuring it. Compliance with the wishes of individuals would be transformed into injustice against the essence of individuals; against their ethical reason which is embodied in ethical relationships.

Finally, we can call it only rashness when States with strict divorce laws (among which the Rhineland is *proud* to be included) are accused by some of hypocrisy. Only a person with a horizon that does not extend beyond the surrounding ethical corruption can venture such accusations, which the Rhineland, for example, finds ridiculous and at most considers as proof that even the notion of ethical relationships can be lost and any ethical fact can be taken as a fairy tale and a lie. This is the immediate consequence of laws that have not been dictated by a high regard for man—a mistake that cannot be eliminated by passing from material contempt to ideal contempt, and by demanding unconscious obedience to supra-ethical and supra-natural authority instead of conscious subordination to ethico-natural forces.

The Community of Women

From *Economic and Philosophic Manuscripts of 1844* (based on the translation by Progress Publishers, Moscow, 1959), pp. 93–95

... COMMUNISM IS:

(1) In its first form only a generalization and consummation of this relationship. It shows itself as such in a twofold form: on the one hand, the dominion of material property bulks so large that it seeks to destroy everything which is not capable of being possessed by all as private property. It seeks to abstract by force from talent, etc. For it the sole purpose of life and existence is direct, physical possession. The category of laborer is not done away with, but extended to all men. The relationship of private property persists as the relationship of the community to the world of things. Finally, this movement of counterposing universal private property to private property finds expression in the bestial form of counterposing to marriage (certainly a form of exclusive private property) the community of women, in which a woman becomes a piece of communal and common property. It may be said that this idea of the community of women gives away the secret of this as yet completely crude and thoughtless communism. Just as the woman passes from marriage to general prostitution,[1] so the entire world of wealth (that is, of man's objective substance) passes from the relationship of exclusive marriage with the owner of private property to a state of universal prostitution with the community. In negating the personality of man in every sphere, this type of communism is really nothing but the logical expression of private property, which is this negation. General envy constituting itself as a power is the disguise in

---

1. Prostitution is only a *specific* expression of the *general* prostitution of the *laborer*, and since it is a relationship in which not the prostitute alone, but also the one who prostitutes, fall—and the latter's abomination is still greater—the capitalist, etc., also comes under this head.—K.M.

which avarice reestablishes itself and satisfies itself, only in another way. The thoughts of every piece of private property—inherent in each piece as such—are at least turned against all wealthier private property in the form of envy and the urge to reduce to a common level, so that this envy and urge even constitute the essence of competition. The crude communism is only the consummation of this envy and of this leveling down proceeding from the preconceived minimum. It has a definite, limited standard. How little this annulment of private property is really an appropriation is in fact proved by the abstract negation of the entire world of culture and civilization, the regression to the unnatural simplicity of the poor and undemanding man who has not only failed to go beyond private property, but has not yet even attained to it.

The community is only a community of labor, and an equality of wages paid out by the communal capital—the community as the universal capitalist. Both sides of the relationship are raised to an imagined universality—labor as a state in which every person is put, and capital as the acknowledged universality and power of the community.

In the approach to woman as the spoil and handmaid of communal lust is expressed the infinite degradation in which man exists for himself, for the secret of this approach has its unambiguous, decisive, plain, and undisguised expression in the relation of man to woman and in the manner in which the direct and natural procreative relationship is conceived. The direct, natural, and necessary relation of person to person is the relation of man to woman. In this natural relationship of the sexes man's relation to nature is immediately his relation to man, just as his relation to man is immediately his relation to nature—his own natural function. In this relationship, therefore, there is sensuously manifested, reduced to an observable fact, the extent to which the human essence has become nature to man, or to which nature has to him become the human essence of man. From this relationship one can therefore judge man's whole level of development. It follows from the character of this relationship how much man as a species being, as man, has come to be himself and to comprehend himself; the relation of man to woman is the most natural relation of human being to human being. It therefore reveals the extent to which man's natural behavior has become human, or the extent to which the human essence in him has come to be nature to him. In this relationship there is revealed, too, the extent to which man's need has become a human need; the extent to which, therefore, the other person as a person has become for him a need—the extent to which he in his individual existence is at the same time a social being. The first positive annulment of private property—crude communism—is thus merely one form in which the vileness of private property, which seeks to set itself up as the positive community, comes to the surface.

Bodies for Sale

From *Economic and Philosophic Manuscripts of 1844*
(Progress Publishers, Moscow, 1959), pp. 111–12

You MUST make everything that is yours *salable*, i.e., useful. If I ask the political economist: Do I obey economic laws if I extract money by offering my body for sale, by surrendering it to another's lust? (The factory workers in France call the prostitution of their wives and daughters the xth working hour, which is literally correct.)—Or am I not acting in keeping with political economy if I sell my friend to the Moroccans? (And the direct sale of men in the form of a trade in conscripts, etc., takes place in all civilized countries.)—Then the political economist replies to me: You do not transgress my laws; but see what Cousin Ethics and Cousin Religion have to say about it. My *political economic* ethics and religion have nothing to reproach you with, but—whom am I now to believe, political economy or ethics? The ethics of political economy is *acquisition*, work, thrift, sobriety—but political economy promises to satisfy my needs. The political economy of ethics is the opulence of a good conscience, of virtue, etc.; but how can I live virtuously if I do not live? And how can I have a good conscience if I am not conscious of anything?

The Condition of Women

From Marx and Engels, *The Holy Family* (written in September-November 1845; published in Frankfurt, 1845), Chapter VIII, Section 6. Translation based on that of Foreign Languages Publishing House, Moscow, 1956

6. REVELATION OF THE MYSTERY OF THE EMANCIPATION OF WOMEN, OR LOUISE MOREL

ON the occasion of the arrest of Louise Morel, Rudolph indulges in reflections which may be abstracted as follows:

"The master often spoils the maid, either by fear, surprise, or other use of the opportunities provided by the nature of the condition of servants. He reduces her to misery, shame, and crime. The law shows no concern for this. . . . The criminal who has practically driven a girl to infanticide is not punished."

Rudolph's reflections do not go so far as to make the condition of servants the object of his most gracious Criticism. Being a petty ruler himself, he is a great advocate of the condition of servants. Still less does he proceed to grasp the general condition of women in modern society as an inhuman one. Faithful in all respects to his previous theory, he objects only to the fact that there is no law to punish a seducer and associate remorse and penance with terrible chastisement.

He only needed to look round at legislation in other countries. English laws fulfill all his wishes. In their delicacy, which Blackstone so highly praises, they go so far as to declare it felony to seduce a prostitute.

Herr Szeliga exclaims with a flourish:

"So" (!)—"thinks" (!)—"Rudolph" (!) "Now compare these thoughts with your fantasies on the emancipation of woman. You can almost feel the fact of that emancipation in them with your hands, but you are too practical by upbringing, and that is why your attempts have failed so often!"

In any case, we must thank Herr Szeliga for revealing the mystery that facts can be felt in thoughts with hands. As for his amusing comparison of Rudolph with men who taught the emancipation of woman, those thoughts should be compared with the following "fantasies" of Fourier's:

"Adultery, seduction, is a credit to the seducer, it is good form. . . . But, poor girl! Infanticide! What a crime! If she prizes her honor she must cut out all traces of dishonor. But if she sacrifices her child to the prejudices of the world her ignominy is all the greater and she is a victim of the prejudices of the law. . . . That is the vicious circle that all the mechanism of civilization describes."

"Is not the young daughter a ware held up for sale to the first bidder who wishes to obtain exclusive ownership of her? . . . Just as in grammar two negations are equal to an affirmation, we can say that in the business of marriage two prostitutions are equal to virtue."

"The change in a historical epoch can always be determined by the progress of women toward freedom, because in the relation of woman to man, of the weak to the strong, the victory of human nature over brutality is most evident. The degree of emancipation of woman is the natural measure of general emancipation."

"The humiliation of the female sex is an essential feature of civilization as well as of barbarity. The only difference is that the civilized system raises to a compound, equivocal, ambiguous, hypocritical mode of existence every vice that barbarity practices in the simple form. . . . Nobody is punished more for keeping woman a slave than man himself" (Fourier).

It is superfluous to compare Rudolph's thoughts with Fourier's masterly characterization of marriage or the works of the materialist section of French communism.

The most wretched offal of socialist literature, a sample of which we find in this novelist, reveal "mysteries" still unknown to Critical Criticism.

The Sanctity of Marriage

From Marx and Engels, *The German Ideology* (written in 1845–46 but not published until 1932); the passages cited below are based on the edition (translated from the German) of Progress Publishers (Moscow, 1964), Chapter III, Section 3 B.

Note 3

As an example of how crime arises from the fixed idea, there is the following:

"The sanctity of marriage is a fixed idea. From sanctity it follows that infidelity is a crime, and therefore a certain law on marriage" (to the great annoyance of the "G[erman chambers" of the "Emperor of all the R[ussias]," not to speak of the "Emperor of Japan" and the "Emperor of China," and particularly the "Sultan") "imposes a more or less long term of punishment for that" (Max Stirner, *Der Einzige und sein Eigenthum* [Leipzig, 1845], p. 269.

Friedrich Wilhelm IV, who thinks he is able to promulgate laws in accordance with the Holy, and therefore is always at loggerheads with the whole world, can comfort himself with the thought that in our Sancho he has found at least one man imbued with faith in the State. Let Saint Sancho just compare the Prussian marriage law, which exists only in the head of its author, with the provisions of the Civil Code which are operative in practice, and he will be able to discover the difference between holy and worldly marriage laws. In the Prussian phantasmagoria, for reasons of State, the sanctity of marriage is supposed to be enforced both upon men and women; in French practice, where the wife is regarded as the private property of her husband, only the wife can be punished for adultery, and then only on the demand of the husband who exercises his property right.

"Blame" for Pauperism

From *The German Ideology* (1845–46), Chapter III, Section 6 B

THE "OPPRESSED" who seeks to lay the "blame" for pauperism on the "State" is, as we saw briefly above, no other that Jacques le bonhomme himself. Secondly, the "oppressed," who comforts himself by causing the "blame" to be laid on the "self-seeking of the rich," is again no other than Jacques le bonhomme. He could have learned something better about the oppressed from the *Facts and Fictions* of John Watts,[1] tailor and doctor of philosophy, from Hobson's *Poor Man's Companion*, etc. And, thirdly, who is the person who should bear the "blame"? Is it, perhaps, the proletarian child who comes into the world tainted with scrofula, who is reared with the help of opium and is sent into the factory when seven years old—or is it, perhaps, the isolated worker who is here expected to "revolt" by himself against the world market—or is it, perhaps, the girl who must either starve or become a prostitute? No, not these but only he who seeks "all the blame," i.e., the "blame" for all the present state of the world "in himself," viz., once again no other than Jacques le bonhomme himself. "This is merely the ancient phenomenon" of Christian heart-searching and doing penance in a German-speculative form, with its idealist phraseology, according to which I, the actual man, do not have to change actuality, which I can only change together with others, but have to change myself in myself.

---

1. John Watts, *The Facts and Fictions of Political Economists* (Manchester, 1842).

Family

From Marx and Engels, *The German Ideology* (1845–46), Chapter III, Section D ("Hierarchy")

ONE CANNOT in general speak of "*the*" family. Historically, the bourgeoisie gives the family the character of the bourgeois family, wherein boredom and money are the binding links, and to which also belongs the bourgeois dissolution of the family, which does not prevent it from constantly continuing its existence. Its dirty existence corresponds to the holy concept of it in official phraseology and universal hypocrisy. Where the family is actually abolished, as in the proletariat, just the opposite of what "Stirner" thinks occurs. There the concept of the family does not exist at all, but here and there, to be sure, family affection, based on extremely real relations, can be found. In the eighteenth century, the concept of the family was dissolved by the philosophers, because the actual family was already in the process of dissolution at the highest pinnacles of civilization. The internal family bond was dissolved, including the separate components constituting the concept of the family, for example, obedience, piety, marital fidelity, etc.; but the real body of the family: property relation, the excluding relation toward other families, forced living together—relations produced by the existence of children, the structure of modern towns, the formation of capital, etc.—remained, although much disturbed, because the existence of the family is made necessary by its connection with the mode of production that is independent of the will of bourgeois society. This indispensability has been strikingly shown during the French Revolution, when for a moment the family was legally as good as abolished. The family continues to

exist even in the nineteenth century, only the process of its dissolution has become more universal, not in regard to concept but
because of the more developed industry and competition; it [the
family] still exists, despite the fact that its dissolution has long been
declared by French and English socialists, and this has at last penetrated
also to the German church fathers by way of French novels.

"Love" and Communism

"Transformation of Communism into Love-daydreams," Marx and Engels in *Circular against Kriege,* Section 1, May 1846.

No. 103 of the *Volks-Tribun*[1] contains an article, "To the Women."
(1) "The women, priestesses of *love.*"
(2) "It is *love* that has been sent to us."
(3) "Apostle of *love.*"
(a) Belletristic intermezzo: "Flaming Glimpses of Humanity," "Tones of Truth."
(b) Hypocritical and ignorant *captatio benevolentiae*[2] of the woman: "Even in the garb of a queen, do not deny the *woman* . . . , also you have not learned to speculate with the tears of the unfortunate; you are too soft to do your best to let the poor child of a *mother* die of hunger."
(4) "The future of the *beloved* child."
(5) "*Beloved* sisters."
(6) "Oh, hear us, you are committing a crime against *love* if you do nothing."
(7) "Of *love.*"
(8) "Of *love.*"
(9) "For the sake of *love.*"
(10) "The most sacred work of *love,* for which we supplicate (whine) you."
(c) Belletristic-Biblical triviality: "The woman is destined to give

---

1. *Der Volks-Tribun,* a German-language weekly of the "true" socialists in New York, edited by Hermann Kriege.
2. Snatching after benevolence.

birth to the son of man," from which it is deduced that men do not give birth to children.

(11) "The holy spirit of community must develop out of the *heart* of LOVE."

(d) Episodical Ave Maria: "*Blessed, three times blessed,* are you women who are selected to give the *first consecration* of the long-promised kingdom of salvation."

(12) "*Beloved* sisters."

(13) "Instead of *love,* hate" (Contrast between bourgeois and communist society).

(14) "You *beloved.*"

(15) "To elevate *love* to the throne."

(16) "Active men in *loving* community."

(17) "True priestess of *love.*"

(e) Esthetic parenthesis: "if your trembling soul has not yet forgotten its beautiful soaring"—(a trick whose feasibility is still to be demonstrated).

(18) "The world of *love.*"

(19) "Kingdom of hate and kingdom of *love.*"

(f) The women are humbugged: "And therefore you have a very weighty voice even in politics. You only have to make use of your influence, and the whole old kingdom of hate sinks into ruins, in order to make room for the new kingdom of *love.*"

(g) Philosophical hush to drown out reflection: "A perpetually cheerful self-employment of all mankind is the end product of your activities."

(20) "Your *love.*" On this occasion, women are asked that their love should "not be small," and "to embrace all people with equal devotion." A demand that is as indecent as it is extravagant.

(h) Fugue: "That thousands upon thousands of deserted orphans are abandoned to horrible murder of conditions." Wherein consists the "horrible"? In that the "orphans" murder the "conditions," or that the "conditions" murder the orphans?

(i) Revelation of the neocommunist policy: "We do not wish to touch the private property of any person; what the usurer has, he may keep. We only want to anticipate the distant robbery of the people's possessions and to prevent Capital from holding back labor's rightful property any longer." This goal is to be attained as follows: "Every poor person is transformed on the spot into a useful member of human society, as soon as he is given the opportunity to become productively active." (Thereby nobody gains greater merit for the "human society" than the capitalists, even those of New York, against whom Kriege blusters so violently). "But this is assured for him forever, as soon as society gives him a piece of land, so that he can feed himself and his family . . . If this immense superficies (the 1,400 million acres of the American national domain) is *withdrawn from commerce and given to labor in limited quantities,* all poverty in America is done away with in *one* stroke; for every man is given the opportunity to establish an inviolable home with his own hands." That it is not within the power of legislators to block by decrees the continuing development of patriarchal conditions into industrial ones, as Kriege wishes, or to throw back the industrial and commercial States of the East Coast of the United States into patriarchal barbarism—such insight was to be expected. For the period before the onset of the above-portrayed splendor, Kriege has prepared the following country parson's words: "And then we can teach men to live *in peace with each other,* to lighten each other's lives and efforts, and:

(21) build on earth the first dwelling of the heaven of *love*" (Piece by piece, 160 acres in size).

Kriege concludes his allocution to the married women as follows: "First turn to

(22) the men of your *love,*

beg them to turn their backs on the old policies . . . , show them your children, adjure them in *your* (the unreasonable ones') *names* to embrace reason." Secondly, to the "maidens": "Let, in

(23) your *lovers,*

the emancipation of the soil be the touchstone of their human worth, and trust not

(24) their *love,*

ere they vowed themselves to mankind" (What does this mean?). When the maidens have borne children, he guarantees them that their children

(25) "would be as *loving*

as you (namely, 'the birds of heaven')," and ends the lyre with the repetition of

(26) "real priestesses of love," "great kingdom of community," and "consecration."

No. 13 of the *Volks-Tribun,* "*Antwort an Sollta*" [Answer to Sollta]:

(27) "He (the great spirit of community) flames as the fire of *love* from the brother's eye."

(28) "What is a woman without a man whom she can *love,* to whom she can surrender her *trembling soul?*"

(29) "All men united in *love.*"

(30) "Mother *love.*"

(31) "*Love* of mankind."

(32) "All the first sounds of *love.*"

(33) "The rays of *love.*"

(k) The goal of communism is: "to subordinate the whole life of mankind to its (the feeling heart's) pulses."

(34) "The tone of *love* flies from the clatter of money."

(35) "With *love* and devotion, everything can be accomplished."

In this *one* issue, we counted no fewer than thirty-five forms of love. This love drivel corresponds to the views of Kriege, who, in his "Answer to Sollta" and elsewhere, presents communism as the loving antithesis of egoism, and reduces a world-historical revolutionary movement to a few words: Love-Hate, Communism-Egoism. This is of a piece with the cowardice with which he flatters the above-mentioned usurer, by promising to leave him what he already possesses, and, further on, promises "not to disturb the *cozy feelings of family life, privacy and folkiness*," but "only to fulfill" them. This cowardly, hypocritical presentation of communism, not as "destruction" but as "the fulfillment" of the existing evil conditions and the illusions which the bourgeois entertain about them, is found throughout all the issues of the *Volks-Tribun*. This hypocrisy and cowardice fits the position he assumes in his discussions with politicians. He recognizes it as a sin against communism (No. 10) if one writes against Catholicizing political fantasists like Lamennais and Börne, while men like Proudhon, Cabet, Dézamy—in a word, all the French communists—are merely persons who "call themselves communists." That the German communists are as far beyond Börne as the French ones are beyond Lamennais, Kriege could already have learned in Germany, Brussels, and London.

What enervating effect these love-daydreams exercises on both sexes, and what massive hysteria and anemia it must call forth among the "maidens," let Kriege himself meditate over.

The Bourgeois Family

From *Manifesto of the Communist Party* (1848),* Part II

ABOLITION of the family. Even the most radical flare up at this infamous proposal of the Communists.

On what foundation is the present family, the bourgeois family, based? On capital, on private gain. In its completely developed form this family exists only among the bourgeoisie. But this state of things finds its complement in the practical absence of the family among the proletarians, and in public prostitution.

The bourgeois family will vanish as a matter of course when its complement vanishes, and both will vanish with the vanishing of capital.

Do you charge us with wanting to stop the exploitation of children by their parents? To this crime we plead guilty.

But, you will say, we destroy the most hallowed of relations when we replace home education by social.

And your education! Is not that also social, and determined by the social conditions under which you educate, by the intervention, direct or indirect, of society by means of schools, etc.? The Communists have not invented the intervention of society in education; they do but seek to alter the character of that intervention, and to rescue education from the influence of the ruling class.

The bourgeois claptrap about the family and education, about the hallowed co-relation of parent and child, becomes all the more disgusting, the more by the action of Modern Industry all family ties among the proletarians are torn asunder, and their children transformed into simple articles of commerce and instruments of labor.

---

* Text in *Karl Marx on Revolution*, Vol. I of The Karl Marx Library, pp. 94–95.

But you Communists would introduce community of women, screams the whole bourgeoisie in chorus.

The bourgeois sees in his wife a mere instrument of production. He hears that the instruments of production are to be exploited in common, and, naturally, can come to no other conclusion than that the lot of being common to all will likewise fall to the women.

He has not even a suspicion that the real point aimed at is to do away with the status of women as mere instruments of production.

For the rest, nothing is more ridiculous than the virtuous indignation of our bourgeois at the community of women which, they pretend, is to be openly and officially established by the Communists. The Communists have no need to introduce community of women; it has existed almost from time immemorial.

Our bourgeois, not content with having the wives and daughters of their proletarians at their disposal, not to speak of common prostitutes, take the greatest pleasure in seducing each others' wives.

Bourgeois marriage is in reality a system of wives in common, and thus, at the most, what the Communists might possibly be reproached with is that they desire to introduce, in substitution for a hypocritically concealed, an openly legalized community of women. For the rest, it is self-evident that the abolition of the present system of production must bring with it the abolition of the community of women springing from that system, i.e, of prostitution both public and private.

Free Education for All Children

From *Manifesto of the Communist Party* (1848)*

Nevertheless, in the most advanced countries the following will be pretty generally applicable: ...

10. Free education for all the children in public schools. Abolition of children's factory labor in its present form. Combination of education with industrial production, etc., etc.

---

* For text, see *Karl Marx on Revolution*, Vol. I of The Karl Marx Library, pp. 97–98.

Unfrequented Schools (I)

From "The Labor Question," in *New-York Daily Tribune,* on November 28, 1853

"Golden opportunities, and the use made of them" is the title of one of the most tragicomical effusions of the grave and profound *Economist.* The "golden opportunities" were, of course, afforded by Free Trade, and the "use" or rather "abuse" made of them refers to the working classes. . . .

"The third use made of the golden opportunity should have been to procure the best possible education for themselves and their children, so as to fit themselves for the improvement in their circumstances, and to learn how to turn it to the best account. Unhappily we are obliged to state that schools have seldom been so ill attended, or school fees so ill paid." Is there anything marvelous in this fact? Brisk trade was synonymous with enlarged factories, with increased application of machinery, with more adult laborers being replaced by women and children, with prolonged hours of work. The more the mill was attended by the mother and the child, the less could the school be frequented. And, after all, of what sort of education would you have given the opportunity to the parents and their children? The opportunity of learning how to keep population at the pace described by Malthus, says *The Economist.* Education, says Mr. Cobden, would show the men that filthy, badly ventilated, overstocked lodgings are not the best means of conserving health and vigor. As well might you save a man from starving by telling him that the laws of Nature demand a perpetual supply of food for the human body. Education, says *The Daily News,* would have informed our working classes how to extract nutritive substance out of dry bones—how to make tea cakes of starch, and how to boil soup with devil's dust.

If we sum up, then, the golden opportunities which have thus been thrown away by the working classes, they consist of the golden opportunity of *not* marrying, of the opportunity of living *less* luxuriously, of *not* asking for higher wages, of becoming capitalists at 15 shillings a week, and of learning how to keep the body together with coarser food, and how to degrade the soul with the pestiferous doctrines of Malthus. . . .

(II)

From "Prosperity—the Labor Question," in *New-York Daily Tribune*, November 30, 1853

... IN MY LAST LETTER,[1] I told the *Economist* that it was not to be wondered at if the working classes had not used the period of prosperity to educate their children and themselves. I am now enabled to forward you the following statement, the names and particulars of which have been given me, and are about to be sent to Parliament: In the last week of September 1852, in the township of _____ four miles from _____, at a bleaching and finishing establishment called _____, belonging to _____, Esq., the undermentioned parties attended their work *sixty hours* consecutively, with the exception of *three hours of rest:*

Girls	Age	Girls	Age	Boys	Age
M.S.	22	H.O.	15	W.G.	9
A.B.	20	M.L.	13	J.K.	10
M.B.	20	B.B.	13		
A.H.	18	M.O.	13		
C.N.	18	A.T.	12		
B.S.	16	C.O.	12		
T.T.	16	S.G.	10!		
M.G.	15	Ann B.	9!		

Boys of nine and ten working sixty hours consecutively, with the exception of three hours' rest! Let the masters say nothing about neglecting education now. One of the above, Ann B., a little girl only nine years of age, fell on the floor, asleep with exhaustion, during the sixty hours; she *was roused and cried, but was forced to resume work!!*

---

1. See "The Labor Question," *Tribune*, November 28, 1853, p. 70.

The factory operatives seem resolved to take the education movement out of the hands of the Manchester humbugs. At a meeting held in the Orchard by the unemployed operatives at Preston, as we hear:

"Mrs. Margaret Fletcher addressed the assembly on the impropriety of married females working in factories and neglecting their children and household duties. Every man was entitled to a fair day's wages for a fair day's work, by which she meant that he ought to have such compensation for the labor as would afford him the means of maintaining himself and family in comfort; of keeping his wife at home to attend to domestic duties, and of educating the children (Cheers)."

Working Children and Irregular
School Attendance

From "Important British Documents," in *New-York Daily Tribune,*
May 20, 1858

... THE THREE CLASSES under the Factory Acts are: (1) Males over
18 years of age, whose labor is unrestricted; (2) males between 13
and 18 years of age, and females above 13 years of age, whose labor
is restricted; (3) children between 8 and 13 years of age, whose labor
is restricted, and who are required to attend school daily. ...

The only restriction upon labor is contained in Par. 22 of the
Print-Works Act (8 and 9 Vict., 29), which enacts that no child between the ages of 8 and 13 years, and no female, shall be employed
during the night, which is defined to be between 10 P.M. and 6 A.M. of
the following morning. Children, therefore, of the age of 8 years, may
be and are lawfully employed in a labor analogous in many respects
to factory labor, mostly in rooms in which the temperature is oppres-
sive, continuously and without any cessation from work for rest or
refreshment, from 6 A.M. till 10 P.M.; and a boy having attained the age
of 13 may, and is often, lawfully employed day and night for any
number of hours, without any restriction whatever. The school attendance of children employed in printing-works is thus provided for:
Every child, before being employed in a print-works, must have attended school for at least thirty days and not less than one hundred
and fifty hours during the six months immediately preceding such
first day of employment, and during the continuance of its employment
in the print-works must attend school for a like period of thirty days and
one hundred fifty hours during every successive period of six months.
The attendance at school must be between 8 A.M. and 6 P.M. No attendance of less than two hours and a half nor more than five hours

on any one day shall be reckoned as part of the one hundred and fifty hours. The philanthropy of the master-printers shines peculiarly in the method of executing these regulations. Sometimes a child would attend school for the number of hours required by law at one period of the day, sometimes at another period, but never regularly; for instance, the attendance on one day might be from 8 A.M. to 11 A.M., on another day from 1 P.M. to 4 P.M., and the child might not appear at school again for several days, when it would attend perhaps from 3 P.M. to 6 P.M.; then it might attend for three or four days consecutively or for a week; then it would not appear in school for three weeks or a month after that, upon some odd days at some odd hours when the employer chose to spare it. Thus the child is as it were buffeted from school to work, and from work to school, until the tale of one hundred and fifty days is told.

Imprisonment of Lady Bulwer-Lytton

From *New-York Daily Tribune*, August 4, 1858 (written, July 23, 1858)

THE GREAT BULWER SCANDAL, which the London *Times* thought to be "fortunately" hushed up by the amicable family arrangement, is far from having subsided into a state of quiescence. It is true that, despite the great party interest involved, the metropolitan press, with some trifling exceptions, did everything in its power to hush the case by a conspiracy of silence—Sir Edward Bulwer being one of the chiefs of the literary coterie which lords it more despotically over the heads of the London journalists than even party connection, and to openly affront the wrath of those whom literary gentlemen lack the necessary courage to defy. The *Morning Post* first informed the public that Lady Bulwer's friends intended insisting upon legal investigation; the London *Times* reprinted the short paragraph of the *Morning Post*, and even the *Advertiser*, although it certainly has no literary position to hazard, did not venture beyond some meager extracts from the *Somerset Gazette*. Even Palmerston's influence proved for the moment unavailing to extort anything from his literary retainers, and on the appearance of the flippantly apologetical letter of Bulwer's son, all these public guardians of the liberty of the subject, while declaring themselves highly satisfied, deprecated any further indelicate intrusion upon the "painful matter." The Tory press, of course, has long since spent all its virtuous indignation on Lord Clanricarde's behalf, and the Radical press, which more or less receives its inspirations from the Manchester School, anxiously avoids creating any embarrassment to the present Administration. Yet, along with the respectable or would-be respectable press of the metropolis, there exists an irrespectable press, absolutely swayed by its political patrons with no literary standing to check them, always ready to coin money out of the privilege of free speech, and anxious to improve an opportunity of appearing in the eyes of the public as the last representatives of manliness. On the other hand, the moral instincts of the bulk of the people once awakened, there will be no need of further maneuvering. The public mind once worked into a state of moral excitement, even the London *Times* may throw off its mask of reserve, and, with a bleeding heart of course, stab the Derby Administration by passing the sentence of "public opinion" on such a literary chieftain even as Sir Edward Lytton Bulwer.

This is exactly the turn things are now taking. That Lord Palmerston, as we hinted at first, is the secret manager of the spectacle is now *un secret qui cours les rues* [a secret which runs through the streets, i.e., an open secret], as the French say. "*On dit* [it is said]," says a London weekly, "that Lady Bulwer Lytton's best friend in this affair has been Lady Palmerston. We all remember how the Tories took up the cudgel for Mr. Norton when Lord Melbourne was in trouble about that gentleman's wife. Tit for tat is fair play. But on reflection it is rather sad at this time of day to find a Secretary of State using the influence of his position to commit acts of oppression, and the wife of a Minister playing off the wife of another Minister against an Administration."

It is often by the crooked ways of political intrigue only that truth becomes smuggled into some corner of the British press. The apparently generous horror at a real outrage is after all but a calculated grimace; and public justice is only appealed to in order to cherish private malice. For aught the chivalrous knights of the inkhorn would care about it, Lady Bulwer might have remained forever in a lunatic asylum at London; she might have been disposed of more quietly than at St. Petersburg or Vienna; the conventionalities of literary decorum would have debarred her from any means of freedom but for the happy circumstance of Palmerston's keen eye singling her out as the thin end of the wedge wherewith possibly to split a Tory Administration.

A short analysis of the letter addressed by Bulwer's son to the London journals will go far to elucidate the true state of the case. Mr. Robert Lytton sets out by asserting that his "simple assertion" must be "at once believed in," because he is "the son of Lady Bulwer Lytton, with the best right to speak on her behalf, and obviously with the best means of information." Now, this very tender son had neither cared for his mother, nor corresponded with her, nor seen her, for nearly seventeen years, until he met her at the hustings at Hertford on the occasion of his father's reelection. When Lady Bulwer left the hustings and visited the Mayor of Hertford in order to apply for the use of the Town Hall as a lecturing room, Mr. Robert B. Lytton sent a physician into the Mayor's house with the mission of taking cognizance of the state of the maternal mind. When, afterward, his mother was kidnapped in London, at the house of Mr. Hale Thompson, Clarges Street, and her cousin, Miss Ryves, ran out into the street, and, seeing Mr. Lytton waiting outside, entreated him to interfere and procure assistance to prevent his mother being carried off to Brentford, Mr. Lytton coolly refused to have anything to do with the matter. Having acted first as one of the principal agents in the plot laid by his father, he now shifts sides and presents himself as the natural spokesman of his mother. The second point pleaded by Mr. Lytton is that his mother "was never for a moment taken to a lunatic asylum," but, on the contrary, into the "private house" of Mr. Robert Gardiner Hill, surgeon. This is a mere quibble. As the "Wyke House," conducted by Mr. Hill, does legally not belong to the category of "asylums," but to that of "Metropolitan Licensed Houses,"[1] it is literally true that Lady Bulwer was thrown, not into a "lunatic asylum," but in a lunatic house.

Surgeon Hill, who trades upon his own account in "lunacy," has also come out with an apology, wherein he states that Lady Bulwer had never been locked in, but, on the contrary, had enjoyed the use of a brougham and driven almost every evening during her detention to Richmond, Acton, Hanworth, or Isleworth. Mr. Hill forgets to tell the public that this "improved treatment of the insane" adopted by him exactly corresponds to the official recommendation of the Commissioners in Lunacy. The friendly grimace, the smiling forbearance, the childish coaxing, the oily twaddle, the knowing winks, and the affected serenity of a band of trained attendants may drive a sensitive woman mad as well as douches, strait waistcoats, brutal keepers and dark wards. However that may be, the protests on the part of Mr. Surgeon Hill and Mr. Lytton amount simply to this, that Lady Bulwer was treated as a lunatic indeed, but after the rules of the new instead of the old system. "I," says Mr. Lytton in his letter, "put myself in constant communication with my mother . . . and I carried out the injunctions of my father, who confided to me implicitly every arrangement . . . and enjoined me to avail myself of the advice of Lord Shaftesbury in whatever was judged best and kindest to Lady Lytton."

Lord Shaftesbury, it is known, is the commander in chief of the host who have their headquarters at Exeter Hall.[2] To deodorize a dirty affair by the odor of sanctity might be considered a *coup de théâtre* worthy of the inventive genius of a novel writer.[3] More than once,

---

1. On England's Asylums and Poor Houses, see Marx's article in the *Tribune*, August 20, 1858.

2. Exeter Hall, London, was the headquarters of the evangelical branch of the Anglican Church from 1831 to 1907.

3. Both Lord Lytton and his wife, Rosina, it happened, were novelists; their son, who became a British diplomat, was also a poet.

in the Chinese business, for instance, and in the Cambridge House conspiracy, Lord Shaftesbury has been employed in that line. Yet Mr. Lytton admits the public only to a half confidence, otherwise he would have plainly declared that on the kidnapping of his mother an impetuous note from Lady Palmerston upset Sir Edward's plans and induced him to "avail himself of the advice of Lord Shaftesbury," who, by a particular mischance, happens to be at once Palmerston's son-in-law and the Chairman of the Commissioners in Lunacy. In his attempt at mystification, Mr. Lytton proceeds to state:

"From the moment my father felt compelled to authorize those steps which have been made the subject of so much misrepresentation, his anxiety was to obtain the opinion of the most experienced and able physicians, in order that my mother should not be subject to restraint for one moment longer than was strictly justifiable. Such was his charge to me."

From the evasive wording of this studiously awkward passage it appears, then, that Sir Edward Bulwer felt the necessity of authoritative medical advice, not for sequestrating his wife as insane, but for setting her free as *mentis compos* [sane]. In fact the medical men upon whose consent Lady Bulwer was kidnapped were anything but "most experienced and able physicians." The fellows employed by Sir Edward were one Mr. Ross, a city apothecary, whom, it seems, his license for trading in drugs has all at once converted into a psychological luminary, and one Mr. Hale Thompson, formerly connected with the Westminster Hospital, but a thorough stranger to the scientific world. It was only after gentle pressure from without had set in, when Sir Edward felt anxious to retrace his steps, that he addressed himself to men of medical standing. Their certificates are published by his son— but what do they prove? Dr. Forbes Winslow, the editor of *The Journal of Psychological Medicine*, who had previously been consulted by Lady Bulwer's legal advisers, certifies that "having examined Lady B. Lytton as to her state of mind," he found it such as "to justify her liberation from restraint." The thing to be proved to the public was, not that Lady Bulwer's liberation, but, on the contrary, that her restraint, was justified. Mr. Lytton dares not touch upon this delicate and decisive point. Would not a constable accused of illegal imprisonment of a free-born Briton be laughed at for pleading that he had committed no wrong in setting his prisoner at large? But is Lady Bulwer really set at large? "My mother," continues Mr. Lytton, "*is now with me, free from all restraint, and about, at her own wish, to travel for a short time, in company with myself and a female friend and relation, of her own selection.*"

Mr. Lytton's letter is dated "No. 1 Park Lane," that is, from the town residence of his father. Has, then, Lady Bulwer been removed from a place of confinement at Brentford to a place of confinement at London and been boldly delivered up to an exasperated foe? Who warrants her "being free from all restraint"? At all events, when signing the proposed compromise, she was not free from restraint, but smarting under Surgeon Hill's improved system. The most important circumstance is this: While Sir Edward has spoken, Lady Bülwer has kept silence. No declaration on her part, given as she is to literary exercise,[4] has met the public eye. An account written by herself, of her own treatment, has been cleverly withdrawn from the hands of the individual to whom it was addressed.

Whatever may be the agreement entered upon by the husband and the wife, the question for the British public is whether, under the cloak of the lunacy act, *lettres de cachet* [warrants for imprisonment, used in France before the Revolution of 1789] may be issued by unscrupulous individuals able to pay tempting fees to two hungry practitioners. Another question is whether a Secretary of State will be allowed to condone for a public crime by a private compromise. It has now oozed out that during the present year, while investigating into the state of a Yorkshire asylum, the Lunacy Commissioners discovered a man, in the full possession of his mental faculties, who, for several years, had been immured and secreted in a cellar. On a question being put in the House of Commons by Mr. Fitzroy in regard to this case, Mr. Walpole answered that he had found "no record of the fact," an answer which denies the record but not the fact. That things will not be allowed to rest at this point may be inferred from Mr. Tite's notice that "on an early day next session he would move for a select committee to inquire into the operation of the Lunacy Act."

---

4. Lady Bulwer-Lytton was the author of a novel, *Cheveley, or the Man of Honour,* which she published in 1839, at the age of thirty-seven.

Evasions of the School Laws (I)

From "The State of British Manufactures," in *New-York Daily Tribune*,
March 15, 1859*

THE FACTORY INSPECTORS of England, Scotland, and Ireland, having
issued their regular half-yearly reports, ending October 31, 1858, on their
different districts, I send you my usual abstract of those most important industrial bulletins. The joint report is this time condensed into
a few lines, and states only that, with the single exception of Scotland,
the encroachments of the manufacturers upon the legal time for the
employment of young persons and women, and especially upon the
time reserved for their meals, are rapidly increasing. They consequently
feel it incumbent upon themselves to urge that these evasions of the
law should be prevented by an amending act. . . .

. . . I willingly embrace the opportunity of paying my respects to
those British factory inspectors, who, in the teeth of all-powerful class
interests, have taken up the protection of the downtrodden multitude
with a moral courage, a steadfast energy, and an intellectual superiority
of which there are not to be found many parallels in these times of
mammon worship.

The first report proceeds from Mr. Leonard Horner, whose district comprises the industrial center of England, the whole of Lancashire, parts of Cheshire, Derbyshire, the West Riding of Yorkshire, the North Riding and the four northern counties of England.
The factory laws being still the object of unmitigated opposition on
the part of the manufacturers, and almost every year witnessing a
parliamentary campaign in favor of their repeal, Mr. Horner starts

* Much of this material was later used in the appropriate section of *Capital;* see
pp. 97-100 of this volume.

with an apology for the legislation which exempted children and women from the absolute sway of the inexorable laws of Free Trade. . . .

It is principally in Mr. Horner's district that willful and deliberate violations of the enactments that restrict the hours of work, as well as those respecting the age of the workers and the attendance to school of children from eight to thirteen years, who by law are to work half-time only, have been on the increase since the recent improved state of trade. . . .

The second report, drawn up by Sir John Kincaid, extends over the whole of Scotland, where, as he states, the laws which regulate the employment of women, young persons, and children in factories continue to be strictly observed. The same is not true in respect of the educational enactments, since it seems with Scotch manufacturers a pet device to obtain for their juvenile workers school certificates from shops put up for that purpose, but where the children do not attend at all, or if they attend, are unfit to gather any instruction. It may suffice to quote two cases. In 1858, Sir John Kincaid, accompanied by Mr. Campbell, the Sub-Inspector, attended two schools from which children employed in some of the Glasgow print-works are used to receive their certificates. I quote from the report:

> The first school was that of Mrs. Ann Killin, in Smith's Court, Bridgeton; there were no children in the schoolroom when we called, and on asking Mrs. Killin to spell her name, she blundered by commencing with the letter C, but presently corrected herself and said it began with K. However, on looking at her signature in the children's school certificate books, I noticed that she did not always spell her name the same, while the character of the writing showed that she was quite incapable of keeping the register. The second school visited was that of William Logue, of Landressey Street, Calton, whose certificates I also felt it my duty to annul. The school apartment was about fifteen feet long and ten feet wide, within that space we counted seventy-five children, screaming something unintelligible at the top of their voices. I requested the schoolmaster to point some of the children out to me, and from the manner in which he surveyed the crowd, I saw that he had no knowledge whether or not any of them were present.

In fact, the educational clauses of the Factory Laws, while they require children to have certificates of school attendance, do not require that they shall have learned anything. . . .

(II)

From "The State of British Manufactures," in *New-York Daily Tribune*, March 24, 1859

I PROPOSE now giving notice of the two Factory Reports alluded to in a former letter.[1] The first is written by Mr. A. Redgrave, whose factory district comprises Middlesex (in and about London), Surrey, Essex, parts of Cheshire, Derbyshire, and Lancashire, and the East Riding (Yorkshire). There were caused during the half year terminated on October 31, 1858, 331 accidents by machinery, of which 12 proved fatal. Mr. Redgrave's report turns almost exclusively on one point, viz: the educational enactments for factories and print-works. Previous to the permanent employment of a child or young person in a factory or print-works, the mill occupier is required to obtain a certificate from the certifying surgeon, who, by virtue of 7 Vict., c. 15, sch. A,* is bound to refuse that certificate if the person presented has "not the ordinary strength and appearance of a child of at least eight years of age, or of a young person of at least thirteen years of age, or if it be incapacitated by disease and bodily infirmity from working daily in the factory for the time allowed by law." Children between the ages of eight and thirteen years are legally disqualified for full-time employment, and have part of their time to give to school attendance, the surgeon being authorized to tender them half-time certificates only. Now it appears from Mr. Redgrave's report that, on the one hand, the parents, if they can obtain full-time wages for their children, are anxious to withdraw them from school and half wages, while the only thing the mill-owner

---

* 7th year of Victoria's reign, June 1844; Chapter 15, Schedule A of a law passed in that year.

1. See "The State of British Manufactures," in *Tribune*, March 15, 1859, p. 81.

looks for in the juvenile hands is strength to enable them to perform their respective work. While the parent seeks full-time wages, the manufacturer seeks the full-time worker. The following advertisement, which appeared in the local newspaper of an important manufacturing town in Mr. Redgrave's district, and which smacks strangely of the slave trade, will show how the mill-owners conform to the provisions of the law, literally:

> Wanted—From 12 to 20 BOYS, not younger than *what will pass for* 13 years of age..............Wages 4s. per week.

In point of fact, the employer is legally not bound to procure a certificate of the children's ages from an authentic source, but an *opinion*, relying upon appearance. The half-time system founded upon the principle that child labor should not be permitted unless, concurrently with such employment, the child attend some school daily, is objected to by the manufacturers on two grounds. They object to their responsibility of enforcing the school attendance of the half-times (children under 13 years of age), and they find it cheaper and less troublesome to employ one set of children instead of two sets, working alternately 6 hours. The first result, therefore, of the introduction of the half-time system was the nominal diminution to nearly one half the children under 13 years employed in factories. From 56,455, to which their number amounted in 1835, it had sunk to 29,283 in 1838. This diminution, however, was to a great extent nominal only, since the complaisance of the certifying surgeons worked a sudden revolution in the respective ages of the juvenile hands of the United Kingdom. At the same ratio, therefore, that the certifying surgeons were more strictly watched by factory inspectors and sub-inspectors, and that the facility of ascertaining the real age of the children from the Registrars of Births increased, a movement opposite to that of 1838 set in. From 29,283, to which the number of children under 13 years of age employed in factories had fallen in 1838, it rose again to 35,122 in 1850, and to 46,071 in 1856, the latter legal return being still far from exhibiting the real proportion of such employment. On the one hand, many of the certifying surgeons know still how to baffle the surveillance of the inspectors, and on the other, many thousand children were withdrawn from school and the half-time system at 11 years of age, by the alteration of the law with respect to silk mills, "a sacrifice which" as one of the factory inspectors says, "may have been accommodating to the mill occupiers, but which has proved injurious to the social interests of the silk districts." Although we may consequently infer that the number of children between 8 and 13 years now employed in the factories and print-works of the

United Kingdom exceeds the number similarly employed in 1835, there can exist no doubt that the half-system had a great share in stimulating inventions for the suppression of child labor. Thus Mr. Redgrave states:

> In fact, one class of manufacturers—the spinners of woolen yarns —now rarely employ children under 13 years of age (i.e., half-time). They have introduced improved and new machinery of various kinds, which altogether supersedes the necessity for the employment of children. For instance, I will mention one process, as an illustration of this diminution, in the number of children, wherein, by the addition of an apparatus called a piecing machine to existing machines, the work of six or four half-times, according to the peculiarity of each machine, can be performed by one young person.

How modern industry, in old-settled countries at least, tends to press children into moneymaking employment has been again illustrated by recent instances in Prussia. The factory law of Prussia of 1835 enacted that after the last of July, 1855, no child should be employed for more than 6 hours per day, and must attend school at least 3 hours per day. This law met with such opposition from the manufacturers that the Government had to give way and enforce it, not throughout Prussia, but by way of experiment in Elberfeld and Barmen only, two contiguous manufacturing towns containing a large manufacturing population engaged in spinning, calico-printing, etc. In the Annual Report of the Chamber of Commerce for Elberfeld and Barmen for 1856, the following representations on this subject are made to the Prussian Government:

> The increase of the rate of labor, as also the increased price of coals and all materials necessary for those branches of manufacture, such as leather, oil, metal, etc., has proved highly disadvantageous to the trade. In addition to this, the strict enforcement of the law of May 1, 1853, concerning the employment of children in the manufactories, has worked very prejudicially. Not only has it caused the withdrawal of a number of children, but it has been rendered impossible to give them that early instruction calculated to render them skillful workmen. In consequence of the lack of these youthful hands, the machines in several establishments were brought to a standstill, as the handling of them could not be performed by grown-up persons. A modification of this law is recommended so as to shorten the forced attendance at school of children who have reached a certain standard of knowledge, as being a measure advantageous to numerous families and to the owners of manufactories.

Women and Ladies

From "English Humanity and America," in *Die Presse* (Vienna),
June 20, 1862

HUMANITY IN ENGLAND, like liberty in France, has now become an
article of export for the traders in politics. We recall the time when
Tsar Nicholas had Polish ladies flogged by soldiers and Lord Palmerston
found the moral indignation of a few parliamentarians over the event
to be "impolitical." We recall that about a decade ago a revolt broke
out on the Ionian Islands which induced the English governor there
to have a not inconsiderable number of Greek women flogged.
Probatum est [It is approved], said Palmerston and his Whig colleagues who were then in office. Only a few years ago official documents of Parliament showed that the tax collectors in India employed
coercive means against the wives of the ryots, the infamy of which
forbids further detailing. Palmerston and colleagues, to be sure, did
not dare to justify these atrocities, but what an outcry they would
have made if a *foreign* government had dared to proclaim publicly its
indignation over these English infamies and to indicate in no uncertain terms that it would intervene if Palmerston and colleagues did not
immediately disavow the Indian tax officials. But Cato the Censor
himself could not watch over the morals of the Roman citizens more
anxiously than the English aristocrats and their ministers do over the
"humanity" of the war-waging Yankees.

The ladies of New Orleans, yellow beauties tastelessly decked out in
jewels and somewhat comparable to the women of the ancient Mexi-
cans, except that they do not devour their slaves *in natura*, are this
time—previously it was the harbors of Charleston—the occasion of a
British-aristocratic display of humanity. The English women (they

are, however, not ladies, nor do they own slaves) who are starving in Lancashire have hitherto inspired no parliamentary utterance; the cry of distress of the Irish women who, with the progressive elimination of the small tenant farmers in green Erin, are thrown half naked into the street and hunted from house to house as if the Tartars had invaded, has hitherto called forth a single echo from Lords, Commons, and Her Majesty's Government—homilies on the absolute rights of landed property. But the ladies of New Orleans!

This, of course, is another matter. These ladies were far too enlightened to participate in the tumult of war, like the goddesses of Olympus, or to cast themselves into the flames, like the women of Saguntum.[1] They have invented a new and undangerous mode of heroism, one that could have been invented only by female slaveholders, and especially in a land where the free portion of the population consists of shopkeepers by vocation, tradesmen in cotton or sugar or tobacco, and does not keep slaves, like the *cives* [citizens] of the world of antiquity. After their men had run away from New Orleans or had crept into their back closets, these ladies rushed into the streets to spit in the faces of the victorious Union troops or to stick out their tongues at them or, like Mephistopheles, in general to make "an indecent gesture," accompanied by insulting words. These Megaeras believed they could be ill-bred "with impunity."

This was their heroism. General Butler[2] issued a proclamation in which he notified them that they would be treated as streetwalkers if they continued to act like streetwalkers. Butler, indeed, has the makings of a lawyer,[3] but seems not to have properly studied English statute law. Otherwise, by analogy with the laws imposed by Castlereagh on Ireland,[4] he would have forbidden them to set foot on the street at all. Butler's warning to the "ladies" of New Orleans has aroused such moral indignation in Earl Carnarvon, Sir J. Wals (who played so ridiculous and hateful a role in Ireland), and Mr. Gregory, who was already demanding recognition of the Confederacy a year ago, that the Earl in the Upper House, and the knight and the man "without a handle to his name" in the Lower House, interpellated the ministry with a view to inquiring what step it intended to take in the name of insulted "humanity." Russell and Palmerston both castigated Butler, both expected that the government in Washington would disavow him, and the very softhearted Palmerston—who be-

---

1. In 219 A.D., after Hannibal captured the besieged Spanish city of Saguntum, the inhabitants incinerated themselves.
2. Benjamin Franklin Butler, military commander of New Orleans in 1862.
3. Butler was a successful Massachusetts lawyer before the Civil War.
4. In 1801 Castlereagh's government instituted martial law in Ireland, after having suppressed an Irish uprising that began in 1798.

hind the back of the Queen, without the foreknowledge of his colleagues, merely out of "human" admiration, recognized the *coup d'état* of December 1851[5] (when "ladies" were actually shot dead, while others were raped by Zouaves)—this same sensitive Viscount declared Butler's warning to be an "infamy." Indeed, ladies—and ladies who actually own slaves—were not even to be allowed to vent their anger and their malice on common Union troops, peasants, artisans, and other rabble with impunity! It is "infamous."

In the public here [in London], nobody is deceived by this humanity farce. It is meant partly to bring forth and partly to strengthen the sentiment for intervention, on the part of France in the first place....

---

5. Louis Bonaparte's *coup d'état* of December 2, 1851, through which he made himself Emperor Napoleon III.

The Apprenticeship System

From "The State of British Manufacturing Industry," in *New-York Daily Tribune*, August 6, 1860

IN THE INFANCY of the factory system, when manufacturers were in want of labor, it was obtained directly by application to the overseers of some distant parish, who forwarded a certain number of apprentices, children of tender age, who were bound to the manufacturers for a term of years. The children being once apprenticed, the Poor Law officers congratulated their respective parishes on their deliverance from idle mouths, while the manufacturer proceeded to make the best of his bargain by keeping them at the most economical rate, and by screwing from them all the labor of which they were capable. Hence the first of the series of Factory Acts passed in 1802, 42 Geo. III., Cap. 73, has for its title "An act for the preservation of the health and morals of apprentices and others employed in cotton and other mills, and cotton and other factories" and was merely intended to mitigate the evils of the apprenticeship system. But as improvements were made in machinery, a different kind of labor was wanted, when trade became brisk and the population of the neighborhood failed to supply the mills with their full complement of hands. These manufacturers sent to Ireland, and brought over Irish families; but Ireland has ceased to be the market from which a supply of labor can be procured on English demand, and manufacturers have now to look to the southern and western counties of England and Wales for families that can be tempted by the present rate of wages in the northern counties to commence a new career of industry. Agents have been sent throughout the country to set forth the advantages offered to families by removing to the manufacturing districts, and they are empowered to make ar-

rangements for the emigration to the north. Many families are said to
have been forwarded by these agents. Still, the importation into a
manufacturing town of a man with his wife and family has this peculiar
disadvantage, that while the younger members of the family, who can
soon be taught and whose services become valuable in a comparatively
short period, are most in request, there is no ready demand for the
labor of the man and his wife, unskilled in factory labor. This has
induced some manufacturers to return, in some measure, to the old
apprenticeship system, and to enter into engagements for specific
periods, with boards of guardians, for the labor of destitute pauper
children. In these cases, the manufacturer lodges, clothes, and feeds the
children, but pays them no regular wages. With the return to this
system complaints of its abuse seem also to have revived. However, this
kind of labor, it should be remembered, would only be sought after
when none other could be procured, for it is a high-priced labor. The
ordinary wages of a boy of 13 would be about 4 shillings per week;
but to lodge, to clothe, to feed, and to provide medical attendance
and proper superintendence for 50 or 100 of these boys, and to set
aside some remuneration for them, could not be accomplished for 4
shillings a head per week.

Juvenile and Child Labor

Karl Marx, "Instructions for the Delegates of the Provisional General Council [of the First International]. The Different Questions." Written in English at the end of August 1866; published in *The International Courier*, February 20 and March 13, 1867

WE CONSIDER the tendency of modern industry to make children and juvenile persons of both sexes cooperate in the great work of social production as a progressive, sound, and legitimate tendency, although under capital it was distorted into an abomination. In a rational state of society *every child whatever*, from the age of 9 years, ought to become a productive laborer in the same way that no able-bodied adult person ought to be exempted from the general law of nature, viz.: to work in order to be able to eat, and work not only with the brain but with the hands too.

However, for the present, we have only to deal with the children and young persons of both sexes [belonging to the working people. They ought to be divided]* into three *classes*, to be treated differently; the first class to range from 9 to 12; the second, from 13 to 15 years; and the third to comprise of ages of 16 and 17 years. We propose that the employment of the first class in any workshop or housework be legally restricted to *two;* that of the second, to *four;* and that of the third, to *six* hours. For the third class, there must be a break of at least one hour for meals or relaxation.

It may be desirable to begin elementary school instruction before the age of 9 years; but we deal here only with the most indispensable antidotes against the tendencies of a social system which degrades the working man into a mere instrument for the accumulation of capital,

* These words were omitted in the newspaper text.

and transforms parents by their necessities into slaveholders, sellers of their own children. The *right* of children and juvenile persons must be vindicated. They are unable to act for themselves. It is, therefore, the duty of society to act on their behalf.

If the middle and higher classes neglect their duties toward their offspring, it is their own fault. Sharing the privileges of these classes, the child is condemned to suffer from their prejudices.

The case of the working class stands quite different. The working man is no free agent. In too many cases he is even too ignorant to understand the true interest of his child, or the normal conditions of human development. However, the more enlightened part of the working class fully understands that the future of its class, and, therefore, of mankind, altogether depends upon the formation of the rising working generation. They know that, before everything else, the children and juvenile workers must be saved from the crushing effects of the present system. This can only be effected by converting *social reason* into *social force*, and, under given circumstances, there exists no other method of doing so than through *general laws*, enforced by the power of the state. In enforcing such laws the working class does not fortify governmental power. On the contrary, they transform that power, now used against them, into their own agency. They effect by a general act what they would vainly attempt by a multitude of isolated individual efforts.

Proceeding from this standpoint we say that no parent and no employer ought to be allowed to use juvenile labor except when combined with education.

By education we understand three things.

Firstly: *Mental education.*

Secondly: *Bodily education,* such as is given in schools of gymnastics, and by military exercise.

Thirdly: *Technological training,* which imparts the general principles of all processes of production, and, simultaneously, initiates the child and young person in the practical use and handling of the elementary instruments of all trades.

A gradual and progressive course of mental, gymnastic, and technological training ought to correspond to the classification of the juvenile laborers. The costs of the technological schools ought to be partly met by the sale of their products.

The combination of paid productive labor, mental education, bodily exercise, and polytechnic training will raise the working class far above the level of the higher and middle classes.

It is self-understood that the employment of all persons from [9] and to 17 years (inclusively) in nightwork and all health-injuring trades must be strictly prohibited by law.

Capital

Editorial Note: All selections from *Capital*, first published in English in 1887, are from the text of the third German edition, and, except as noted, as translated by Samuel Moore and Edward Aveling, and edited by Frederick Engels. The text used here was published by Charles H. Kerr & Co., Chicago, 1906, as revised by Ernest Untermann.

Apprentices

From *Capital*, Vol. I, Chapter X, Section 5

WAS NOT Dr. Ure right in crying down the 12 hours' bill of 1833 as a retrogression to the times of the dark ages? It is true these regulations contained in the statute mentioned by Petty[1] apply also to apprentices. But the condition of child labor, even at the end of the seventeenth century, is seen from the following complaint:

> 'Tis not their practice (in Germany) as with us in this kingdom, to bind an apprentice for seven years; three or four is their common standard: and the reason is, because they are educated from their cradle to something of employment, which renders them the more apt and docile, and consequently the more capable of attaining to a ripeness and quicker proficiency in business. Whereas our youth, here in England, being bred to nothing before they come to be apprentices, make a very slow progress and require much longer time wherein to reach the perfection of accomplished artists.[2]

---

1. William Petty, *Political Anatomy of Ireland* (London, 1691).
2. Andrew Ure, *A Discourse on the necessity of encouraging Mechanick Industry* (London, 1689).

Exploitation of Children

From *ibid.*, Vol. I, Chapter 10, Section 5, footnote

MACAULAY, who has falsified history in the interests of the Whigs and the bourgeoisie, declaimed as follows: "The practice of setting children prematurely to work . . . prevailed in the seventeenth century to an extent which, when compared with the extent of the manufacturing system, seems almost incredible. At Norwich, the chief seat of the clothing trade, a little creature of six years old was thought fit for labor. Several writers of that time, and among them some who were considered as eminently benevolent, mentioned with exultation the fact that in that single city boys and girls of very tender age create wealth exceeding what was necessary for their own subsistence by twelve thousand pounds a year. The more carefully we examine the history of the past, the more reason shall we find to dissent from those who imagine that our age has been fruitful of new social evils. . . . That which is new is the intelligence and the humanity which remedies them." (*History of England*, Vol. I, p. 417). Macaulay might have reported further that "extremely well-disposed" *amis du commerce* [friends of commerce] in the seventeenth century narrate with "exultation" how in a poorhouse in Holland a child of four was employed, and that this example of "*vertu mise en pratique*" [virtue put into practice] passes muster in all the writings of humanitarians à la Macaulay up to the time of A. Smith. It is correct that with the emergence of manufacturing, in contrast with handicrafts, traces of exploitation of children begin to appear, an exploitation that to a certain extent had always existed among peasants and was the more developed the more severe the yoke pressed on the countryman. The

tendency of capital is there unmistakable, but the facts themselves
are still as isolated as the phenomenon of two-headed children. Therefore they were noted with "exultation" by the far-seeing *"amis du
commerce"* as particularly worthy of remark and wonder, and were
recommended as models for their own world and for posterity. This
same Scottish sycophant and speechifier Macaulay says: "We hear
today only of retrogression and see only progress." What eyes and,
especially, what ears!

Disgraceful Schools

From *ibid.*, Vol. I, Chapter 15, Section 3

THE MORAL DEGRADATION caused by the capitalistic exploitation of women and children has been so exhaustively depicted by F. Engels in his *Lage der Arbeitenden Klasse Englands*,[1] and other writers, that I need only mention the subject in this place. But the intellectual desolation, artificially produced by converting immature human beings into mere machines for the fabrication of surplus value, a state of mind clearly distinguishable from the natural ignorance which keeps the mind fallow without destroying its capacity for development, its natural fertility, this desolation finally compelled even the English Parliament to make elementary education a compulsory condition to the "productive" employment of children under 14 years, in every industry subject to the Factory Acts. The spirit of capitalist production stands out clearly in the ludicrous wording of the so-called education clauses in the Factory Acts, in the absence of administrative machinery, an absence that again makes the compulsion illusory, in the opposition of the manufacturers themselves to these education clauses, and in the tricks and dodges they put in practice for evading them.

For this the legislature is alone to blame, by having passed a delusive law, which, while it would seem to provide that the children employed in factories shall be *educated*, contains no enactment by which that professed end can be secured. It provides nothing more than the children shall on certain days of the week, and for a certain number of hours (three) in each day, be inclosed within the four walls of a place called a school, and that the employer of the child

1. Frederick Engels, *The Condition of the Working Class in England in 1844* (published in German in 1845 and in English in 1892).

shall receive weekly a certificate to that effect signed by a person designated by the subscriber as a schoolmaster or schoolmistress.[2]

Previous to the passing of the amended Factory Act, 1844, it happened not infrequently that the certificates of attendance at school were signed by the schoolmaster or schoolmistress with a cross, as they themselves were unable to write.

> On one occasion, on visiting a place called a school, from which certificates of school attendance had issued, I was so struck with the ignorance of the master, that I said to him: "Pray, sir, can you read?" His reply was: "Aye, summat!" and as a justification of his right to grant certificates, he added: "At any rate, I am before my scholars." The inspectors, when the Bill of 1844 was in preparation, did not fail to represent the disgraceful state of the places called schools, certificates from which they were obliged to admit as a compliance with the laws, but they were successful only in obtaining thus much, that since the passing of the Act of 1844, the figures in the school certificate must be filled up in the handwriting of the schoolmaster, who must also sign his Christian and surname in full.[3]

Sir John Kincaid, factory inspector for Scotland, relates experiences of the same kind.

> The first school we visited was kept by a Mrs. Ann Killin. Upon asking her to spell her name, she straightway made a mistake, by beginning with the letter C, but correcting herself immediately, she said her name began with a K. On looking at her signature, however, in the school certificate books, I noticed that she spelt it in various ways, while her handwriting left no doubt as to her unfitness to teach. She herself also acknowledged that she could not keep the register. . . . In a second school I found the schoolroom 15 feet long and 10 feet wide, and counted in this space 75 children, who were gabbling something unintelligible.[4]

But it is not only in the miserable places above referred to that the children obtain certificates of school attendance without having received instruction of any value, for in many schools where there is a competent teacher his efforts are of little avail from the distracting crowds of children of all ages, from infants of three years old and upwards; his livelihood, miserable at the best, depending on the pence received from the greatest number of children whom it is possible to cram into the space. To this is to be added scanty school

---

2. L. Horner, in "Reports of Insp. of Fact. for 30th June, 1857," p. 17.
3. L. Horner, in "Rep. of Insp. of Fact. for 31st Oct., 1855," pp. 18, 19.
4. Sir John Kincaid, in "Rep. of Insp. of Fact. for 31st Oct., 1858," pp. 31, 32.

furniture, deficiency of books and other materials for teaching, and the depressing effect upon the poor children themselves of a close, noisome atmosphere. I have been in many such schools, where I have seen rows of children doing absolutely nothing; and this is certified as school attendance, and, in statistical returns, such children are set down as being educated.[5]

In Scotland the manufacturers try all they can to do without the children that are obliged to attend school.

It requires no further argument to prove that the educational clauses of the Factory Act, being held in such disfavor among mill-owners, tend in a great measure to exclude that class of children alike from the employment and the benefit of education contemplated by this Act.[6]

Horribly grotesque does this appear in print-works, which are regulated by a special Act. By that Act,

every child, before being employed in a print-work must have attended school for at least 30 days, and not less than 150 hours, during the six months immediately preceding such first day of employment, and during the continuance of its employment in the print-works it must attend for a like period of 30 days and 150 hours during every successive period of six months. . . . The attendance at school must be between 8 A.M. and 6 P.M. No attendance of less than 2½ hours nor more than 5 hours on any one day shall be reckoned as part of the 150 hours. Under ordinary circumstances the children attend school morning and afternoon for 30 days, for at least 5 hours each day, and upon the expiration of the 30 days the statutory total of 150 hours having been attained, having, in their language, made up their book, they return to the print-works, where they continue until the six months have expired, when another installment of school attendance becomes due, and they again seek the school until the book is again made up. . . . Many boys having attended school for the required number of hours, when they return to school after the expiration of their six months' work in the print-works are in the same condition as when they first attended school as print-works boys, that they have lost all they gained by their previous school attendance. . . . In other print-works the children's attendance at school is made to depend altogether upon the exigencies of the work in the establishment. The requisite number of hours is made up each six months, by installments consisting of from 3 to 5 hours at a time, spreading over, perhaps, the whole six months. . . . For instance, the attendance on one day might be

5. L. Horner, in "Reports, etc., for 31st Oct. 1857," pp. 17, 18.
6. Sir J. Kincaid, in "Reports, etc., 31st Oct., 1856," p. 66.

from 8 to 11 A.M., on another day from 1 P.M. to 4 P.M., and the child might not appear at school again for several days, when it would attend from 3 P.M. to 6 P.M.; then it might attend for 3 or 4 days consecutively, or for a week, then it would not appear in school for 3 weeks or a month, after that upon some odd days at some odd hours when the operative who employed it chose to spare it; and thus the child was, as it were, buffeted from school to work, from work to school, until the tale of 150 hours was told.[7]

By the excessive addition of women and children to the ranks of the workers, machinery at last breaks down the resistance which the male operatives in the manufacturing period continued to oppose to the despotism of capital.

---

7. A. Redgrave, in "Rep. of Insp. of Fact., 31st Oct., 1857," pp. 41–42.

Women and Children in Tile

and Brick-Making

From *ibid.*, Vol. I, Chapter 15, Section 8 c

IN THE HARDWARE MANUFACTURES of Birmingham and the neighborhood, there are employed, mostly in very heavy work, 30,000 children and young persons, besides 10,000 women. There they are to be seen in the unwholesome brass-foundaries, button factories, enameling, galvanizing, and lacquering works.[1] Owing to the excessive labor of their workpeople, both adult and nonadult, certain London houses where newspapers and books are printed have got the ill-omened name of "slaughterhouses."[2] Similar excesses are practiced in bookbinding, where the victims are chiefly women, girls, and children; young persons have to do heavy work in rope walks and night work in salt mines, candle manufactories, and chemical works; young people are worked to death at turning the looms in silk weaving, when it is not carried on by machinery.[3] One of the most shameful, the most dirty, and the worst paid kinds of labor, and one on which women and young girls are by preference employed, is the sorting of rags. It is well known that Great Britain, apart from its own immense store of rags, is the emporium for the rag trade of the whole world. They flow in from Japan, from the most remote States of South America, and from the Canary Islands. But the chief sources of their supply are Germany, France, Russia, Italy, Egypt, Turkey, Belgium, and Holland. They are used for manure, for making bed-flocks, for shoddy, and they

---

1. And now forsooth children are employed at file-cutting in Sheffield.—K.M.

2. Children's Employment Commission. Fifth Report, 1866, p. 3, n. 24; p. 6, n. 55; p. 7, ns. 59, 60.

3. *Loc. cit.*, pp. 114, 115, ns. 6, 7. The commissioner justly remarks that though as a rule machines take the place of men, here literally young persons replace machines.—K.M.

serve as the raw material of paper. The rag sorters are the medium for the spread of smallpox and other infectious diseases, and they themselves are the first victims.[4] A classical example of overwork, of hard and inappropriate labor, and of its brutalizing effects on the workman from his childhood upwards, is afforded not only by coal mining and miners generally, but also by tile- and brick-making, in which industry the recently invented machinery is, in England, used only here and there. Between May and September the work lasts from 5 in the morning till 8 in the evening, and where the drying is done in the open air it often lasts from 4 in the morning till 9 in the evening. Work from 5 in the morning till 7 in the evening is considered "reduced" and "moderate."

Both boys and girls of 6 and even 4 years of age are employed. They work for the same number of hours, often longer, than the adults. The work is hard and the summer heat increases the exhaustion. In a certain tile field at Mosley, e.g., a young woman 24 years of age was in the habit of making 2,000 tiles a day, with the assistance of two little girls, who carried the clay for her, and stacked the tiles. These girls carried daily 10 tons up the slippery sides of the clay pits, from a depth of 30 feet, and then for a distance of 210 feet.

> It is impossible for a child to pass through the purgatory of a tile-field without great moral degradation. . . . The low language, which they are accustomed to hear from their tenderest years, the filthy, indecent, and shameless habits, amidst which, unknowing, and half wild, they grow up, make them in afterlife lawless, abandoned, dissolute. . . . A frightful source of demoralization is the mode of living. Each molder, who is always a skilled laborer, and the chief of a group, supplies his seven subordinates with board and lodging in his cottage. Whether members of his family or not, the men, boys, and girls all sleep in the cottage, which contains generally two, exceptionally three rooms, all on the ground floor, and badly ventilated. These people are so exhausted after the day's work that neither the rules of health or cleanliness, nor of decency are in the least observed. Many of these cottages are models of untidiness, dirt, and dust. . . . The greatest evil of the system that employs young girls on this sort of work consists in this, that, as a rule, it chains them fast from childhood for the whole of their afterlife to the most abandoned rabble. They become rough, foul-mouthed boys, before Nature has taught them that they are women. Clothed in a few dirty rags, the legs naked far above the knees, hair and face besmeared with dirt, they learn to treat all feelings of decency and of shame with contempt. During mealtimes they lie at full

---

4. See the Report on the rag trade, and numerous details in Public Health, VIII Rep., London, 1866, app. pp. 196, 208.

length in the fields, or watch the boys bathing in a neighboring canal. Their heavy day's work at length completed, they put on better clothes, and accompany the men to the public houses.

That excessive insobriety is prevalent from childhood upwards among the whole class is only natural.

The worst is that the brick-makers despair of themselves. You might as well, said one of the better kind to a chaplain of Southallfield, try to raise and improve the devil as a brickie, sir![5]

---

5. Children's Employment Commission, Fifth Report, 1866, xvi, ns. 96, 97, and p. 130, ns. 39, 61. See also Third Report, 1864, pp. 48, 56.

Women and Children Lace Workers
in Domestic Industry

From *ibid.*, Vol. I, Chapter 15, Section 8 d

I NOW COME to the so-called domestic industry. In order to get an idea of the horrors of this sphere, in which capital conducts its exploitation in the background of modern mechanical industry, one must go to the apparently quite idyllic trade of nail-making, carried on in a few remote villages of England. In this place, however, it will be enough to give a few examples from those branches of the lace-making and straw-plaiting industries that are not yet carried on by the aid of machinery, and that as yet do not compete with branches carried on in factories or in manufactories.

Of the 150,000 persons employed in England in the production of lace, about 10,000 fall under the authority of the Factory Act, 1861. Almost the whole of the remaining 140,000 are women, young persons, and children of both sexes, the male sex, however, being weakly represented. The state of health of this cheap material for exploitation will be seen from the following table, computed by Dr. Trueman, physician to the Nottingham General Dispensary. Out of 686 female patients who were lace-makers, most of them between the ages of 17 and 24, the number of consumptive ones were:

1852	1 in 45		1857	1 in 13
1853	1 in 28		1858	1 in 15
1854	1 in 17		1859	1 in 9
1855	1 in 18		1860	1 in 8
1856	1 in 15		1861	1 in 8

. . . The Factory Act of 1861 regulates the actual making of the lace, so far as it is done by machinery, and this is the rule in England. The branches that we are now about to examine, solely with regard to those of the workpeople who work at home, and not those who work in manufactories or warehouses, fall into two divisions, viz. (1) finishing; (2) mending. The former gives the finishing touches to the machine-made lace, and includes numerous subdivisions.

The lace finishing is done either in what are called "Mistresses' Houses" or by women in their own houses, with or without the help of their children. The women who keep the "Mistresses' Houses" are themselves poor. The workroom is in a private house. The mistresses take orders from the manufacturers or from warehousemen, and employ as many women, girls, and young children as the size of their rooms and the fluctuating demand of the business will allow. The number of the workwomen employed in these workrooms varies from 20 to 40 in some, and from 10 to 20 in others. The average age at which the children commence work is six years, but in many cases it is below five. The usual working hours are from 8 in the morning till 8 in the evening, with 1½ hours for meals, which are taken at irregular intervals, and often in the foul workrooms. When business is brisk, the labor frequently lasts from 8 or even 6 o'clock in the morning till 10, 11, or 12 o'clock at night. In English barracks, the regulation space allotted to each soldier is 500–600 cubic feet, and in the military hospitals 1,200 cubic feet. But in those finishing styles there are but 67 to 100 cubic feet to each person. At the same time the oxygen of the air is consumed by gas lights. In order to keep the lace clean, and although the floor is tiled or flagged, the children are often compelled, even in winter, to pull off their shoes.

> It is not at all uncommon in Nottingham to find 14 to 20 children huddled together in a small room, of, perhaps, not more than 12 feet square, and employed for 15 hours out of the 24, at work that of itself is exhausting, from its weariness and monotony, and is besides carried on under every possible unwholesome condition. . . . Even the very youngest children work with a strained attention and a rapidity that is astonishing, hardly ever giving their fingers rest or slowering their motion. If a question be asked them, they never raise their eyes from their work for fear of losing a single moment.

The "long stick" is used by the mistresses as a stimulant more and more as the working hours are prolonged. "The children gradually tire and become as restless as birds toward the end of their long detention at an occupation that is monotonous, eye-straining, and exhausting from the uniformity in the posture of the body. Their work is like slavery."[1] When women and their children work at home, which

---

1. Children's Employment Commission. Second Report (London, 1864), pp. xix, xx, xxi.

nowadays means in a hired room, often in a garret, the state of things is, if possible, still worse. This sort of work is given out within a circle of 80 miles radius from Nottingham. On leaving the warehouses at 9 or 10 o'clock at night, the children are often given a bundle of lace to take home with them and finish. The Pharisee of a capitalist represented by one of his servants accompanies this action, of course, with the unctuous phrase: "That's for mother," yet he knows well enough that the poor children must sit up and help.[2]

Pillow lace-making is chiefly carried on in England in two agricultural districts; one, the Honiton lace district, extending from 20 to 30 miles along the south coast of Devonshire, and including a few places in North Devon; the other comprising a great part of the counties of Buckingham, Bedford, and Northampton, and also the adjoining portions of Oxfordshire and Huntingdonshire. The cottages of the agricultural laborers are the places where the work is usually carried on. Many manufacturers employ upwards of 3,000 of these lace-makers, who are chiefly children and young persons of the female sex exclusively. The state of things described as incidental to lace finishing is here repeated, save that instead of the "Mistresses' Houses," we find what are called "lace-schools," kept by poor women in their cottages. From their fifth year and often earlier, until their twelfth or fifteenth year, the children work in these schools; during the first year the very young ones work from four to eight hours, and later, from six in the morning till eight and ten o'clock at night.

> The rooms are generally the ordinary living rooms of small cottages, the chimney stopped up to keep out drafts, the inmates kept warm by their own animal heat alone, and this frequently in winter. In other cases, these so-called schoolrooms are like small storerooms without fireplaces. . . . The overcrowding in these dens and the consequent vitiation of the air are often extreme. Added to this is the injurious effect of drains, privies, decomposing substances, and other filth usual in the purlieus of the smaller cottages.

With regard to space:

> In one lace-school 18 girls and a mistress, 35 cubic feet to each person; in another, where the smell was unbearable, 18 persons and 24½ cubic feet per head. In this industry are to be found employed children of 2 and 2½ years.[3]

Where lace-making ends in the counties of Buckingham and Bedford, straw-plaiting begins, and extends over a large part of Hertford-

---

2. *Ibid.*, pp. xxi, xxii.
3. *Ibid.*, pp. xxix, xxx.

shire and the westerly and northerly parts of Essex. In 1861 there were 40,043 persons employed in straw-plaiting and straw-hat making; of these, 3,815 were males of all ages, the rest females, of whom 14,913, including about 7,000 children, were under 20 years of age. In the place of the lace-schools we find here the "straw-plait schools." The children commence their instruction in straw-plaiting generally in their fourth year. Education, of course, they get none. The children themselves call the elementary schools "natural schools," to distinguish them from these blood-sucking institutions, in which they are kept at work simply to get through the task, generally 30 yards daily, prescribed by their half-starved mothers. These same mothers often make them work at home, after school is over, till 10, 11, and 12 o'clock at night. The straw cuts their mouths, with which they constantly moisten it, and their fingers. Dr. Ballard gives it as the general opinion of the whole body of medical officers in London that 300 cubic feet is the minimum space proper for each person in a bedroom or workroom. But in the straw-plait schools space is more sparingly allotted than in the lace-schools, "12⅔, 17, 18½ and below 22 cubic feet for each person." The smaller of these numbers, says one of the commissioners, Mr. White, represents less space than the half of what a child would occupy if packed in a box measuring 3 feet in each direction. Thus do the children enjoy life till the age of 12 or 14. The wretched half-starved parents think of nothing but getting as much as possible out of their children. The latter, as soon as they are grown up, do not care a farthing, and naturally so, for their parents, and leave them. "It is no wonder that ignorance and vice abound in a population so brought up. . . . Their morality is at the lowest ebb . . . a great number of the women have illegitimate children, and that at such an immature age that even those most conversant with criminal statistics are astounded."[4] And the native land of these model families is the pattern Christian country for Europe; so says at least Count Montalembert, certainly a competent authority on Christianity!

Wages in the above industries, miserable as they are (the maximum wages of a child in the straw-plait schools rising in rare cases to 3 shillings), are reduced far below their nominal amount by the prevalence of the truck system everywhere, but especially in the lace districts.[5]

---

4. *Ibid.*, pp. xl, xli.
5. *Ibid.*, First Report, 1863, p. 185.

Women and Children in the Apparel Industry: The Sewing Machine Revolution

From *ibid.*, Section e

THE CHEAPENING OF LABOR POWER, by sheer abuse of the labor of women and children, by sheer robbery of every normal condition requisite for working and living, and by the sheer brutality of over-work and night work, meets at last with natural obstacles that cannot be overstepped. So also, when based on these methods, do the cheapening of commodities and capitalist exploitation in general. So soon as this point is at last reached—and it takes many years—the hour has struck for the introduction of machinery, and for the thenceforth rapid conversion of the scattered domestic industries and also of manufactures into factory industries.

An example, on the most colossal scale, of this movement is afforded by the production of wearing apparel. This industry, according to the classification of the Children's Employment Commission, comprises straw-hat makers, ladies'-hat makers, cap-makers, tailors, milliners and dressmakers, shirt-makers, corset-makers, glove-makers, shoemakers, besides many minor branches, such as the making of neckties, collars, etc. In 1861, the number of females employed in these industries, in England and Wales, amounted to 586,299; of these, 115,242 at the least were under 20, and 16,650 under 15 years of age. The number of these workwomen in the United Kingdom in 1861 was 750,334. The number of males employed in England and Wales in hat-making, shoe-making, glove-making and tailoring was 437,969; of these, 14,964 under 15 years, 89,285 between 15 and 20, and 333,117 over 20 years. Many of the smaller branches are not included in these figures. But take the figures as they stand; we then have for England and Wales alone, according to the census of 1861, a total of 1,024,277 persons, about as many as are absorbed by agriculture and cattle breeding. We begin to understand what becomes of the immense quantities of goods conjured up by the magic of machinery, and of the enormous masses of work-people, which that machinery sets free.

The production of wearing apparel is carried on partly in manu-factories in whose workrooms there is but a reproduction of that division of labor, the *membra disjecta* of which were found ready to hand; partly by small master-handicraftsmen; these, however, do not, as formerly, work for individual consumers but for manu-factories and warehouses, and to such an extent that often whole towns and stretches of country carry on certain branches, such as shoemaking, as a specialty; finally, on a very great scale by the so-called domestic workers, who form an external department of the manufactories, ware-houses, and even the workshops of the smaller masters.[1]

The raw material, etc., is supplied by mechanical industry, the mass of cheap human material (*taillable à merci et miséricorde*)[2] is composed of the individuals "liberated" by mechanical industry and improved agriculture. The manufactures of this class owed their origin chiefly to the capitalist's need to have at hand an army ready equipped to meet any increase of demand.[3] . . . At last the critical point was reached. The basis of the old method, sheer brutality in the exploitation of the workpeople accompanied more or less by a systematic division of labor, no longer sufficed for the expanding markets and for the still more rapidly expanding competition of the capitalists. The hour struck for the advent of machinery. The decisively revolutionary ma-chine, the machine which attacks in an equal degree the whole of the numberless branches of this sphere of production—dressmaking, tailor-ing, shoemaking, sewing, hat-making, and many others—is the sewing machine.

Its immediate effect on the workpeople is like that of all machinery, which, since the rise of modern industry, has seized upon new branches of trade. Children of too tender an age are sent adrift. The wage of the machine hands rises compared with that of the houseworkers, many of whom belong to the poorest of the poor. That of the better-situated handicraftsmen, with whom the machine competes, sinks. The new machine hands are exclusively girls and young women. With the help of mechanical force they destroy the monopoly that male labor had of

---

1. In England millinery and dressmaking are for the most part carried on on the premises of the employer, partly by workmen who live there, partly by women who live off the premises.—K.M.
2. Delivered to mercy and charity.
3. Mr. White, a commissioner, visited a military clothing manufactory that employed 1,000 to 1,200 persons, almost all females, and a shoe manufactory with 1,300 persons; of these nearly one half were children and young persons.—K.M.

the heavier work, and they drive off from the lighter work numbers of old women and very young children. The overpowering competition crushes the weakest of the manual laborers. The fearful increase in death from starvation during the last ten years in London runs parallel with the extension of machine sewing.[4] The new workwomen turn the machines by hand and foot, or by hand alone, sometimes sitting, sometimes standing, according to the weight, size, and special make of the machine, and expend a great deal of labor power. Their occupation is unwholesome, owing to the long hours, although in most cases they are not so long as under the old system. Wherever the sewing machine locates itself in narrow and already overcrowded workrooms, it adds to the unwholesome influences. "The effect," says Mr. Lord, "on entering low-ceiled workrooms in which 30 to 40 machine hands are working is unbearable. . . . The heat, partly due to the gas stoves used for warming the irons, is horrible. . . . Even when moderate hours of work, i.e., from 8 in the morning till 6 in the evening, prevail in such places, yet 3 or 4 persons fall into a swoon regularly every day."[5]

---

4. An instance. The weekly report of deaths by the Registrar-General, dated 26th February, 1864, contains 5 cases of death from starvation. On the same day *The Times* reports another case. Six victims of starvation in one week!—K.M.

5. Children's Employment Commission, Second Report, 1864, p. lxvii, n. 406–09; p. 84, n. 124; p. lxxiii, n. 441; p. 68, n. 6; p. 84, n. 126; p. 78, n. 85; p. 76, n. 69; p. lxxii, n. 483.

Elementary Education and Children
in Factories

From *ibid.*, Vol. 1, Chapter 15, Section 9

FACTORY LEGISLATION, that first conscious and methodical reaction of society against the spontaneously developed form of the process of production, is, as we have seen, just as much the necessary product of modern industry as cotton yarn, self-acting machines, and the electric telegraph. ...

Paltry as the education clauses of the [Factory] Act appear on the whole, yet they proclaim elementary education to be an indispensable condition to the employment of children.[1] The success of those clauses proved for the first time the possibility of combining education and gymnastics[2] with manual labor, and, consequently, of combining manual labor with education and gymnastics. The factory inspectors soon found out by questioning the schoolmasters that the factory children, although receiving only one half the education of the regular day scholars, yet learned quite as much and often more.

---

1. According to the English Factory Act, parents cannot send their children under 14 years of age into Factories under the control of the Act unless at the same time they allow them to receive elementary education. The manufacturer is responsible for compliance with the Act. "Factory education is compulsory, and it is a condition of labor." ("Rep. Insp. Fact., 31st October 1865," p. 111.)

2. On the very advantageous results of combining gymnastics (and drilling in the case of boys) with compulsory education for factory children and pauper scholars, see the speech of N. W. Senior at the seventh annual congress of "The National Association for the Promotion of Social Science," in "Report of Proceedings, &c.," Lond. 1863, pp. 63, 64; also the "Rep. Insp. Fact., 31st October, 1865," pp. 118, 119, 120, 126, sqq.

This can be accounted for by the simple fact that, with only being at school for one half of the day, they are always fresh, and nearly always ready and willing to receive instruction. The system on which they work, half manual labour, and half school, renders each employment a rest and a relief to the other; consequently, both are far more congenial to the child than would be the case were he kept constantly at one. It is quite clear that a boy who has been at school all the morning cannot (in hot weather particularly) cope with one who comes fresh and bright from his work.[3]

Further information on this point will be found in Senior's speech at the Social Science Congress at Edinburgh in 1863. He there shows, amongst other things, how the monotonous and uselessly long school hours of the children of the upper and middle classes uselessly add to the labor of the teacher, "while he not only fruitlessly but absolutely injuriously wastes the time, health, and energy of the children."[4] From the factory system budded, as Robert Owen has shown us in detail, the germ of the education of the future, an education that will, in the case of every child over a given age, combine productive labor with instruction and gymnastics, not only as one of the methods of adding to the efficiency of production, but as the only method of producing fully developed human beings.

Modern Industry, as we have seen, sweeps away by technical means the manufacturing division of labor, under which each man is bound hand and foot for life to a single detail operation. At the same time, the capitalistic form of that industry reproduces this same division of labor in a still more monstrous shape; in the factory proper, by converting the workman into a living appendage of the machine; and every-

---

3. "Rep. Insp. Fact. 31st Oct., 1865," p. 118. A silk manufacturer naively states to the Children's Employment Commissioners: "I am quite sure that the true secret of producing efficient workpeople is to be found in uniting education and labor from a period of childhood. Of course the occupation must not be too severe, nor irksome, or unhealthy. But of the advantage of the union I have no doubt. I wish my own children could have some work as well as play to give variety to their schooling." ("Ch. Empl. Comm. V. Rep.," p. 82, n. 36.)

4. Senior, loc. cit., p. 66. How Modern Industry, when it has attained to a certain pitch, is capable, by the revolution it effects in the mode of production and in the social conditions of production, of also revolutionizing people's minds is strikingly shown by a comparison of Senior's speech in 1863 with his philippic against the Factory Act of 1833; or by a comparison of the views of the congress above referred to with the fact that in certain country districts of England poor parents are forbidden, on pain of death by starvation, to educate their children. Thus, e.g., Mr. Snell reports it to be a common occurrence in Somersetshire that, when a poor person claims parish relief, he is compelled to take his children from school. Mr. Wollarton, the clergyman at Feltham, also tells of cases where all relief was denied to certain families "because they were sending their children to school!"

where outside the factory,[5] partly by reestablishing the division of labor on a fresh basis by the general introduction of the labor of women and children, and of the cheap unskilled labor.

The antagonism between the manufacturing division of labor and the methods of Modern Industry makes itself forcibly felt. It manifests itself, amongst other ways, in the frightful fact that a great part of the children employed in modern factories and manufactures are from their earliest years riveted to the most simple manipulations and exploited for years without being taught a single sort of work that would afterwards make them of use, even in the same manufactory or factory. In the English letter-press printing trade, for example, there existed formerly a system, corresponding to that in the old manufactures and handicrafts, of advancing the apprentices from easy to more and more difficult work. They went through a course of teaching till they were finished printers. To be able to read and write was for every one of them a requirement of their trade. All this was changed by the printing machine. It employs two sorts of laborers, one grown up, tenters, the other, boys mostly from 11 to 17 years of age whose sole business is either to spread the sheets of paper under the machine or to take from it the printed sheets. They perform this weary task, in London especially, for 14, 15, and 16 hours at a stretch, during several days in the week, and frequently for 36 hours, with only 2 hours' rest for meals and sleep.[6] A great part of them cannot read, and they are, as a rule, utter savages and very extraordinary creatures.

> To qualify them for the work which they have to do, they require no intellectual training; there is little room in it for skill, and less for judgment; their wages, though rather high for boys, do not increase proportionately as they grow up, and the majority of them cannot look for advancement to the better-paid and more responsible post of machine minder, because while each machine has but one minder, it has at least two, and often four, boys attached to it.[7]

5. Wherever handicraft machines, driven by men, compete directly or indirectly with more developed machines driven by mechanical power, a great change takes place with regard to the laborer who drives the machine. At first the steam engine replaces this laborer, afterwards he must replace the steam engine. Consequently the tension and the amount of labor power expended become monstrous, and especially so in the case of the children who are condemned to this torture. Thus Mr. Longe, one of the commissioners, found in Coventry and the neighborhood boys of from 10 to 15 years employed in driving the ribbon looms, not to mention younger children who had to drive smaller machines. "It is extraordinarily fatiguing work. The boy is a mere substitute for steam power." ("Ch. Empl. Comm. V. Rep. 1866," p. 114, n. 6.) As to the fatal consequences of "this system of slavery," as the official report styles it, see *loc. cit.*, pp. 114 sqq.

6. *Loc. cit.*, p. 3, n. 24.

7. *Loc. cit.*, p. 7, n. 60.

As soon as they get too old for such child's work, that is about 17 at the latest, they are discharged from the printing establishments. They become recruits of crime. Several attempts to procure them employment elsewhere were rendered of no avail by their ignorance and brutality, and by their mental and bodily degradation.

As with the division of labor in the interior of the manufacturing workshops, so it is with the division of labor in the interior of society. So long as handicraft and manufacture form the general groundwork of social production, the subjection of the producer to one branch exclusively, the breaking up of the multifariousness of his employment,[8] is a necessary step in the development. On that groundwork each separate branch of production acquires empirically the form that is technically suited to it, slowly perfects it, and, so soon as a given degree of maturity has been reached, rapidly crystallizes that form. The only thing that here and there causes a change, besides new raw material supplied by commerce, is the gradual alteration of the instruments of labor. But their form, too, once definitely settled by experience, petrifies, as is proved by their being in many cases handed down in the same form by one generation to another during thousands of years. A characteristic feature is, that, even down into the eighteenth century, the different trades were called "mysteries" (*mystères*);[9] into their secrets none but those duly initiated could penetrate. Modern Industry rent the veil that concealed from men their own social process of production, and that turned the various spontaneously divided branches of production into so many riddles, not only to outsiders, but even to the initiated. The principle which is pursued, of resolving each process into its constituent movements, without any regard to their possible execution by the hand of man, created the new modern science of technology. The varied, apparently unconnected, and petrified forms of the industrial processes now resolved themselves into so many conscious and systematic applications of natural science to the

---

8. "In some parts of the Highlands of Scotland, not many years ago, every peasant, according to the Statistical Account, made his own shoes of leather tanned by himself. Many a shepherd and cottar too, with his wife and children, appeared at church in clothes which had been touched by no hands but their own, since they were shorn from the sheep and sown in the flaxfield. In the preparation of these, it is added, scarcely a single article had been purchased, except the awl, needle, thimble, and a very few parts of the ironwork employed in the weaving. The dyes, too, were chiefly extracted by the women from trees, shrubs and herbs." (Dugald Stewart's "Works," Hamilton Ed., Vol. VIII, pp. 327–28.)

9. In the celebrated *Livre des métiers* of Etienne Boileau, we find it prescribed that a journeyman on being admitted among the masters had to swear "to love his brethren with brotherly love, to support them in their respective trades, not willfully to betray the secrets of the trade, and besides, in the interests of all, not to recommend his own wares by calling the attention of the buyer to defects in the articles made by others."

attainment of given useful effects. Technology also discovered the few main fundamental forms of motion, which, despite the diversity of the instruments used, are necessarily taken by every productive action of the human body; just as the science of mechanics sees in the most complicated machinery nothing but the continual repetition of the simple mechanical powers.

Modern Industry never looks upon and treats the existing form of a process as final. The technical basis of that industry is therefore revolutionary, while all earlier modes of production were essentially conservative.[10] By means of machinery, chemical processes and other methods, it is continually causing changes not only in the technical basis of production, but also in the functions of the laborer, and in the social combinations of the labor process. At the same time, it thereby also revolutionizes the division of labor within the society, and incessantly launches masses of capital and of workpeople from one branch of production to another. But if Modern Industry, by its very nature, therefore necessitates variation of labor, fluency of function, universal mobility of the laborer, on the other hand, in its capitalistic form, it reproduces the old division of labor with its ossified particularizations. We have seen how this absolute contradiction between the technical necessities of Modern Industry, and the social character inherent in its capitalistic form, dispels all fixity and security in the situation of the laborer; how it constantly threatens, by taking away the instruments of labor, to snatch from his hands his means of subsistence,[11] and, by suppressing his detail function, to make him superfluous. We have seen, too, how this antagonism vents its rage in the creation of that monstrosity, an industrial reserve army, kept in misery in order to be always at the disposal of capital; in the incessant human sacrifices from among the working class, in the most reckless squandering of labor power, and in the devastation caused by a social anarchy which turns every economic progress into a social calamity. This is

---

10. "The bourgeoisie cannot exist without continually revolutionizing the instruments of production, and thereby the relations of production and all the social relations. Conservation, in an unaltered form, of the old modes of production was on the contrary the first condition of existence for all earlier industrial classes. Constant revolution in production, uninterrupted disturbance of all social conditions, everlasting uncertainty and agitation, distinguish the bourgeois epoch from all earlier ones. All fixed, fast-frozen relations, with their train of ancient and venerable prejudices and opinions, are swept away, all new formed ones become antiquated before they can ossify. All that is solid melts into air, all that is holy is profaned, and man is at last compelled to face with sober senses his real conditions of life, and his relations with his kind." (F. Engels and Karl Marx: *Communist Manifesto*, London, 1848, p. 5.)

11. "You take my life.
When you do take the means whereby I live."
Shakespeare.

the negative side. But if, on the one hand, variation of work at present imposes itself after the manner of an overpowering natural law, and with the blindly destructive action of a natural law that meets with resistance[12] at all points, Modern Industry, on the other hand, through its catastrophes imposes the necessity of recognizing, as a fundamental law of production, variation of work, consequently fitness of the laborer for varied work, consequently the greatest possible development of his varied aptitudes. It becomes a question of life and death for society to adapt the mode of production to the normal functioning of this law. Modern Industry, indeed, compels society, under penalty of death, to replace the detail worker of today, crippled by lifelong repetition of one and the same trivial operation, and thus reduced to the mere fragment of a man, by the fully developed individual, fit for a variety of labors, ready to face any change of production, and to whom the different social functions he performs are but so many modes of giving free scope to his own natural and acquired powers.

One step already spontaneously taken toward effecting this revolution is the establishment of technical and agricultural schools, and of *"écoles d'enseignement professionnel,"* in which the children of the workingmen receive some little instruction in technology and in the practical handling of the various implements of labor. Though the Factory Act, that first and meager concession wrung from capital, is limited to combining elementary education with work in the factory, there can be no doubt that when the working class comes into power, as inevitably it must, technical instruction, both theoretical and practical, will take its proper place in the working-class schools. There is also no doubt that such revolutionary ferments, the final result of which is the abolition of the old division of labor, are diametrically opposed to the capitalistic form of production, and to the economic status of the laborer corresponding to that form. But the historical development of the antagonisms, immanent in a given form of production, is the only way in which that form of production can be dissolved and a new form established. "Ne sutor ultra crepidam"—this nec plus ultra of handicraft wisdom became sheer nonsense from the moment the

---

12. A French workman, on his return from San Francisco, writes as follows: "I never could have believed, that I was capable of working at the various occupations I was employed on in California. I was firmly convinced that I was fit for nothing but letter-press printing. . . . Once in the midst of this world of adventurers, who change their occupation as often as they do their shirt, egad, I did as the others. As mining did not turn out remunerative enough, I left it for the town, where in succession I became typographer, slater, plumber, &c. In consequence of thus finding out that I am fit for any sort of work. I feel less of a mollusk and more of a man." (A. Corbon, "De l'enseignement professionnel," 2ème ed., p. 50.)

watchmaker Watt invented the steam engine, the barber Arkwright the throstle, and the working jeweller, Fulton, the steamship.[13]

So long as Factory legislation is confined to regulating the labor in factories, manufactures, etc., it is regarded as a mere interference with the exploiting rights of capital. But when it comes to regulating the so-called "home labor,"[14] it is immediately viewed as a direct attack on the *patria potestas*, on parental authority. The tender-hearted English Parliament long affected to shrink from taking this step. The force of facts, however, compelled it at last to acknowledge that modern industry, in overturning the economic foundation on which was based the traditional family, and the family labor corresponding to it, had also unloosed all traditional family ties. The rights of the children had to be proclaimed. The final report of the Ch. Empl. Comm. of 1866, states: "It is, unhappily, to a painful degree apparent throughout the whole of the evidence, that against no persons do the children of both sexes so much require protection as against their parents." The system of unlimited exploitation of children's labor in general and the so-called home labor in particular is "maintained only because the parents are able, without check or control, to exercise this arbitrary and mischievous power over their young and tender offspring. . . . Parents must not possess the absolute power of making their children mere 'machines to earn so much weekly wage.' . . . The children and young persons, therefore, in all such cases may justifiably claim from the legislature, as a natural right, that an exemption should be secured to them, from what destroys prematurely their physical strength, and lowers them in the scale of intellectual and moral beings."[15] It was not, however, the misuse of parental authority that created the capitalistic exploitation, whether direct or indirect, of children's labor; but, on the contrary, it was the capitalistic mode of exploitation which, by sweep-

---

13. John Bellers, a very phenomenon in the history of Political Economy, saw most clearly at the end of the seventeenth century the necessity for abolishing the present system of education and division of labor, which beget hypertrophy and atrophy at the two opposite extremities of society. Amongst other things he says this: "An idle learning being little better than the learning of idleness . . . Bodily labor, it's a primitive institution of God. . . . Labor being as proper for the bodies' health as eating is for its living; for what pains a man saves by ease, he will find in disease. . . . Labor adds oil to the lamp of life, when thinking inflames it. . . . A childish, silly employ" (a warning this, by presentiment, against the Basedows and their modern imitators) "leaves the children's minds silly." ("Proposals for Raising a Colledge of Industry of all Useful Trades and Husbandry." London, 1696, pp. 12, 14, 18.)

14. This sort of labor goes on mostly in small workshops, as we have seen in the lace-making and straw-plaiting trades, and as could be shown more in detail from the metal trades of Sheffield, Birmingham, etc.

15. "Ch. Empl. Comm., V. Rep.," p. xxv, n. 162, and II. Rep., p. xxxviii, ns. 285, 289, pp. xxv, xxvi, n. 191.

ing away the economic basis of parental authority, made its exercise degenerate into a mischievous misuse of power. However terrible and disgusting the dissolution, under the capitalist system, of the old family ties may appear, nevertheless, modern industry, by assigning as it does an important part in the process of production, outside the domestic sphere, to women, to young persons, and to children of both sexes, creates a new economic foundation for a higher form of the family and of the relations between the sexes. It is, of course, just as absurd to hold the Teutonic-Christian form of the family to be absolute and final as it would be to apply that character to the ancient Roman, the ancient Greek, or the Eastern forms which, moreover, taken together form a series in historical development. Moreover, it is obvious that the fact of the collective working group being composed of individuals of both sexes and all ages must necessarily, under suitable conditions, become a source of humane development; although in its spontaneously developed, brutal, capitalistic form, where the laborer exists for the process of production, and not the process of production for the laborer, that fact is a pestiferous source of corruption and slavery.[16]

The necessity for a generalization of the Factory Acts, for transforming them from an exceptional law relating to mechanical spinning and weaving—those first creations of machinery—into a law affecting social production as a whole, arose, as we have seen, from the mode in which Modern Industry was historically developed. In the rear of that industry, the traditional form of manufacture, of handicraft, and of domestic industry, is entirely revolutionized; manufactures are constantly passing into the factory system, and handicrafts into manufactures; and lastly, the spheres of handicraft and of the domestic industries became, in a, comparatively speaking, wonderfully short time, dens of misery in which capitalistic exploitation obtains free play for the wildest excesses. There are two circumstances that finally turn the scales: first, the constantly recurring experience that capital, so soon as it finds itself subject to legal control at one point, compensates itself all the more recklessly at other points;[17] secondly, the cry of the capitalists for equality in the conditions of competition, i.e., for equal restraint on all exploitation of labor.[18] On this point let us listen to two heartbroken cries. Messrs. Cooksley of Bristol, nail and chain, etc., manufacturers, spontaneously introduced the regulations of the Factory Act into their business. "As the old irregular system prevails in neighboring works, the Messrs. Cooksley are subject to the disadvantage of having their boys enticed to continue their labor elsewhere after 6 P.M.

---

16. "Factory labor may be as pure and excellent as domestic labor, and perhaps more so." ("Rep. Insp. Fact., 31st October, 1865," p. 129.)

17. "Rep. Insp. of Fact., 31st October, 1865," pp. 27–32.

18. Numerous instances will be found in "Rep. of Insp. of Fact."

'This,' they naturally say, 'is an injustice and loss to us, as it exhausts a portion of the boy's strength, of which we ought to have the full benefit.' "[19] Mr. J. Simpson (paper box and bag maker, London) states before the commissioners of the Ch. Empl. Comm.: "He would sign any petition for it" (legislative interference). . . . "As it was, he always felt restless at night, when he had closed his place, lest others should be working later than him and getting away his orders."[20] Summarizing, the Ch. Empl. Comm. says:

> It would be unjust to the larger employers that their factories should be placed under regulation while the hours of labor in the smaller places in their own branch of business were under no legislative restriction. And to the injustice arising from the unfair conditions of competition, in regard to hours, that would be created if the smaller places of work were exempt, would be added the disadvantage to the larger manufacturers of finding their supply of juvenile and female labor drawn off to the places of work exempt from legislation. Further, a stimulus would be given to the multiplication of the smaller places of work, which are almost invariably the least favorable to the health, comfort, education, and general improvement of the people.[21]

In its final report the Commission proposes to subject to the Factory Act more than 1,400,000 children, young persons, and women, of which number about one half are exploited in small industries and by the so-called home work.[22] It says,

> But if it should seem fit to Parliament to place the whole of that large number of children, young persons, and females under the protective legislation above adverted to . . . it cannot be doubted that such legislation would have a most beneficent effect, not only upon the young and the feeble, who are its more immediate objects, but upon the still larger body of adult workers, who would in

---

19. "Ch. Empl. Comm., V. Rep.," p. x, n. 35.
20. "Ch. Empl. Comm., V. Rep.," p. ix, n. 28.
21. *Loc. cit.*, p. xxv, ns. 165–167. As to the advantages of large-scale, compared with small-scale, industries, see "Ch. Empl. Comm., III. Rep.," p. 13, n. 144, p. 25, n. 121, p. 26, n. 125, p. 27, n. 140, etc.
22. The trades proposed to be brought under the Act were the following: Lace-making, stocking-weaving, straw-plaiting, the manufacture of wearing apparel with its numerous subdivisions, artificial flower-making, shoe-making, hat-making, glove-making, tailoring, all metal works, from blast furnaces down to needleworks, etc., paper mills, glassworks, tobacco factories, india-rubber works, braid-making (for weaving), hand-carpet-making, umbrella and parasol making, the manufacture of spindles and spools, letter-press printing, bookbinding, manufacture of stationery (including paper bags, cards, colored paper, etc.), rope-making, manufacture of jet ornaments, brick-making, silk manufacture by hand, Coventry weaving, saltworks, tallow chandlers, cement works, sugar refineries, biscuit-making, various industries connected with timber, and other mixed trades.

all these employments, both directly and indirectly, come immediately under its influence. It would enforce upon them regular and moderate hours; it would lead to their places of work being kept in a healthy and cleanly state; it would therefore husband and improve that store of physical strength on which their own well-being and that of the country so much depends; it would save the rising generation from that overexertion at an early age which undermines their constitutions and leads to premature decay; finally, it would ensure them—at least up to the age of 13—the opportunity of receiving the elements of education, and would put an end to that utter ignorance . . . so faithfully exhibited in the Reports of our Assistant Commissioners, and which cannot be regarded without the deepest pain, and a profound sense of national degradation.[23]

The Tory* Cabinet announced in the Speech from the Throne, on February 5, 1867, that it had framed the proposals of the Industrial Commission of Inquiry[24] into Bills. To get that far, another twenty years of *experimentum in corpore vili* had been required. Already in 1840 a Parliamentary Commission of Inquiry on the labor of children had been appointed. Its Report, in 1842, unfolded, in the words of Nassau W. Senior,

> the most frightful picture of avarice, selfishness and cruelty on the part of masters and of parents, and of juvenile and infantile misery, degradation and destruction ever presented. . . . It may be supposed that it describes the horrors of a past age. But there is unhappily evidence that those horrors continue as intense as they were. A pamphlet published by Hardwicke about two years ago states that the abuses complained of in 1842 are in full bloom at the present day. It is a strange proof of the general neglect of the morals and health of the children of the working class, that this report lay unnoticed for 20 years, during which the children, "bred up without the remotest sign of comprehension as to what is meant by the term morals, who had neither knowledge, nor religion, nor natural affection," were allowed to become the parents of the present generation.[25]

---

* Here (from "The Tory Cabinet. . . ." to "Nassau W. Senior") the English text has been altered in conformity with the 4th German edition.—*Ed.*

23. *Loc. cit.,* p. xxv, n. 169.

24. The Factory Acts Extension Act was passed on August 12, 1867. It regulates all foundries, smithies, and metal manufactories, including machine shops; furthermore glassworks, paper mills, gutta-percha and india-rubber works, tobacco manufactories, letter-press printing and bookbinding works, and, lastly, all workshops in which more than 50 persons are employed. The Hours of Labor Regulation Act, passed on August 17, 1867, regulates the smaller workshops and the so-called domestic industries.

25. Senior, "Social Science Congress," pp. 55–58.

The social conditions having undergone a change, Parliament could not venture to shelve the demands of the Commission of 1862, as it had done those of the Commission of 1840. Hence in 1864, when the Commission had not yet published more than a part of its reports, the earthenware industries (including the potteries), makers of paper hangings, matches, cartridges, and caps, and fustian cutters were made subject to the Acts in force in the textile industries. In the Speech from the Throne on 5th February, 1867, the Tory Cabinet of the day announced the introduction of Bills founded on the final recommendations of the Commission, which had completed its labors in 1866.

On the 15th August, 1867, the Factory Acts Extension Act, and on the 21st August, the Workshops' Regulation Act, received the Royal Assent; the former Act having reference to large industries, the latter to small.

The former applies to blast furnaces, iron and copper mills, foundries, machine shops, metal manufactories, gutta-percha works, paper mills, glassworks, tobacco manufactories, letter-press printing (including newspapers), bookbinding, in short to all industrial establishments of the above kind, in which 50 individuals or more are occupied simultaneously, and for not less than 100 days during the year.

To give an idea of the extent of the sphere embraced by the Workshops' Regulation Act in its application, we cite from its interpretation clause the following passages:

Handicraft shall mean any manual labor exercised by way of trade, or for purposes of gain in, or incidental to, the making any article or part of an article, or in, or incidental to, the altering, repairing, ornamenting, finishing, or otherwise adapting for sale any article.

Workshop shall mean any room or place whatever in the open air or under cover, in which any handicraft is carried on by any child, young person, or woman, and to which and over which the person by whom such child, young person, or woman is employed, has the right of access and control.

Employed shall mean occupied in any handicraft, whether for wages or not, under a master or under a parent as herein defined.

Parent shall mean parent, guardian, or person having the custody of, or control over, any . . . child or young person.

Clause 7, which imposes a penalty for employment of children, young persons, and women contrary to the provisions of the Act, subjects to fines not only the occupier of the workshop, whether parent or not, but even "the parent of, or the person deriving any direct benefit from the labor of, or having the control over, the child, young person or woman."

The Factory Acts Extension Act, which affects the large establishments, derogates from the Factory Act by a crowd of vicious exceptions and cowardly compromises with the masters.

The Workshops' Regulation Act, wretched in all its details, remained a dead letter in the hands of the municipal and local authorities who were charged with its execution. When, in 1871, Parliament withdrew from them this power, in order to confer it on the Factory Inspectors, to whose province it thus added by a single stroke more than one hundred thousand workshops, and three hundred brickworks, care was taken at the same time not to add more than eight assistants to their already undermanned staff.[26]

What strikes us, then, in the English legislation of 1867, is, on the one hand the necessity imposed on the parliament of the ruling classes of adopting in principle measures so extraordinary, and on so great a scale, against the excesses of capitalistic exploitation; and on the other hand, the hesitation, the repugnance, and the bad faith with which it lent itself to the task of carrying those measures into practice.

The Inquiry Commission of 1862 also proposed a new regulation of the mining industry, an industry distinguished from others by the exceptional characteristic that the interests of landlord and capitalist there join hands. The antagonism of these two interests had been favorable to Factory legislation, while on the other hand the absence of that antagonism is sufficient to explain the delays and chicanery of the legislation on mines.

The Inquiry Commission of 1840 had made revelations so terrible, so shocking, and creating such a scandal all over Europe, that to salve its conscience Parliament passed the Mining Act of 1842, in which it limited itself to forbidding the employment underground in mines of children under 10 years of age and females.

Then another Act, the Mines' Inspecting Act of 1860, provides that mines shall be inspected by public officers nominated specially for that purpose, and that boys between the ages of 10 and 12 years shall not be employed unless they have a school certificate, or go to school for a certain number of hours. This Act was a complete dead letter owing to the ridiculously small number of inspectors, the meagerness of their powers, and other causes that will become apparent as we proceed.

One of the most recent Blue books on mines is the "Report from the

---

26. The "personnel" of this staff consisted of 2 inspectors, 2 assistant inspectors, and 41 subinspectors. Eight additional subinspectors were appointed in 1871. The total cost of administering the Acts in England, Scotland, and Ireland amounted for the year 1871–72 to no more than £25,347, inclusive of the law expenses incurred by prosecutions of offending masters.

Select Committee on Mines, together with etc. Evidence, 23rd July, 1866." This Report is the work of a Parliamentary Committee selected from members of the House of Commons, and authorized to summon and examine witnesses. It is a thick folio volume in which the Report itself occupies only five lines to this effect; that the committee has nothing to say, and that more witnesses must be examined!

The mode of examining the witnesses reminds one of the cross-examination of witnesses in English courts of justice; where the advocate tries, by means of impudent, unexpected, equivocal and involved questions, put without connection, to intimidate, surprise, and confound the witness, and to give a forced meaning to the answers extorted from him. In this inquiry the members of the committee themselves are the cross-examiners, and among them are to be found both mine-owners and mine exploiters; the witnesses are mostly working coal miners. The whole farce is too characteristic of the spirit of capital not to call for a few extracts from this Report. For the sake of conciseness I have classified them. I may also add that every question and its answer are numbered in the English Blue books.

I. Employment in mines of boys of 10 years and upwards. In the mines the work, inclusive of going and returning, usually lasts 14 or 15 hours, sometimes even from 3, 4 and 5 o'clock A.M., till 5 and 6 o'clock P.M. (ns. 6, 452, 83). The adults work in two shifts, of eight hours each; but there is no alternation with the boys, on account of the expense (ns. 80, 203, 204). The younger boys are chiefly employed in opening and shutting the ventilating doors in the various parts of the mine; the older ones are employed on heavier work, in carrying coal, etc. (ns. 122, 739, 1747). They work these long hours underground until their 18th or 22nd year, when they are put to miner's work proper (n. 161). Children and young persons are at present worse treated, and harder worked than at any previous period (ns. 1663–1667). The miners demand almost unanimously an act of Parliament prohibiting the employment in mines of children under 14. And now Hussey Vivian (himself an exploiter of mines) asks: "Would not the opinion of the workman depend upon the poverty of the workman's family?" Mr. Bruce: "Do you not think it would be a very hard case, where a parent had been injured, or where he was sickly, or where a father was dead, and there was only a mother, to prevent a child between 12 and 14 earning 1s. 7d. a day for the good of the family? . . . You must lay down a general rule? . . . Are you prepared to recommend legislation which would prevent the employment of children under 12 and 14, whatever the state of their parents might be?" "Yes." (ns. 107–110). Vivian: "Supposing that an enactment were passed preventing the employment of children under the age of 14, would it not be probable that . . . the parents of children would seek employment for their children in other directions, for instance, in manufacture?" "Not generally I think" (n. 174). Kinnaird: "Some of the boys are keepers of doors?" "Yes." "Is there not generally a very great draught every time you open a door or close it?" "Yes, generally there is." "It sounds a very easy thing, but it is in fact rather a painful one?" "He is imprisoned there just the same as if he was in a cell of a jail." Bourgeois Vivian: "Whenever a boy is furnished with a lamp cannot he read?" "Yes, he can read, if he finds himself in candles. . . . I suppose he would be found fault with if he were discovered reading; he is there to mind his business, he has a duty to perform, and he has to attend to it in the first place, and I do not think it would be allowed down the pit " (ns. 139, 141, 143, 158, 160).

II. Education.—The working miners want a law for the compulsory education of their children, as in factories. They declare the clauses of the Act of 1860, which require a school certificate to be obtained before employing boys of 10 and 12 years of age, to be quite illusory. The examination of the witnesses on this subject is truly droll. "Is it (the Act) required more against the masters or against the parents?" "It is required against both I think." "You cannot say whether it is required against one more than against the other?" "No; I can hardly answer that question." (ns. 115, 116). "Does there appear to be any desire on the part of the employers that the boys should have such hours as to enable them to go to school?" "No; the hours are never shortened for that purpose." (n. 137.) Mr. Kinnaird: "Should you say that the colliers generally improve their education; have you seen instances of men who have, since they began to work, greatly improved their education, or do they not rather go back, and lose any advantage that they may have gained?" "They generally become worse: they do not improve; they acquire bad habits; they get on to drinking and gambling and such-like, and they go completely to wreck." (n. 211.) "Do they make any attempt of the kind (for providing instruction) by having schools at night?" "There are few collieries where night schools are held, and perhaps at those collieries a few boys do go to those schools; but they are so physically exhausted that it is to no purpose that they go there." (n. 454.) "You are then," concludes the bourgeois, "against education?" "Most certainly not; but," etc. (n. 443.) "But are they (the employers) not compelled to demand them (school certificates)?" "By law they are; but I am not aware that they are demanded by the employers." "Then it is your opinion that this provision of the Act as to requiring certificates is not generally carried out in the collieries?" "It is not carried out." (ns. 443, 444.) "Do the men take a great interest in this question (of education)?" "The majority of them do." (n. 717.) "Are they very anxious to see the law enforced?" "The majority are." (n. 718.) "Do you think that in this country any law that you pass ... can really be effectual unless the population themselves assist in putting it into operation?" "Many a man might wish to object to employing a boy, but he would perhaps become marked by it." (n. 720.) "Marked by whom?" "By his employers." (n. 721.) "Do you think that the employers would find any fault with a man who obeyed the law...?" "I believe they would." (n. 722.) "Have you ever heard of any workman objecting to employ a boy between 10 and 12, who could not write or read?" "It is not left to men's option." (n. 123.) "Would you call for the interference of Parliament?" "I think that if anything effectual is to be done in the education of the colliers' children, it will have to be made compulsory by Act of Parliament." (n. 1634.) "Would you lay that obligation upon the colliers only, or all the workpeople of Great Britain?" "I came to speak for the colliers." (n. 1636.) "Why should you distinguish them (colliery boys) from other boys?" "Because I think they are an exception to the rule." (n. 1638.) "In what respect?" "In a physical respect." (n. 1639.) "Why should education be more valuable to them than to other classes of lads?" "I do not know that it is more valuable; but through the overexertion in mines there is less chance for the boys that are employed there to get education, either at Sunday schools, or at the day schools." (n. 1640). "It is impossible to look at a question of this sort absolutely by itself?" (n. 1644). "Is there a sufficiency of schools?"—"No". . . . (n. 1646). "If the State were to require that every child should be sent to school, would there be schools for the children to go to?" "No; but I think if the circumstances were to spring up, the schools would be forthcoming." (n. 1647). "Some of them (the boys) cannot read and write at all, I suppose?" "The majority cannot. . . . The majority of the men themselves cannot." (ns. 705, 725.)

Children in Favorable Climates

From *ibid.*, Vol. I, Chapter 16

APART FROM the degree of development, greater or less, in the form of social production, the productiveness of labor is fostered by physical conditions. These are all referable to the constitution of man himself (race, etc.), and to surrounding nature. The external physical conditions fall into two great economic classes, (1) Natural wealth in means of subsistence, i.e., a fruitful soil, waters teeming with fish, etc., and (2) natural wealth in the instruments of labor, such as waterfalls, navigable rivers, wood, metal, coal, etc. At the dawn of civilization, it is the first class that turns the scale; at a higher stage of development, it is the second. Compare, for example, England with India, or, in ancient times, Athens and Corinth with the shores of the Black Sea.

Schools in Basel

From "Report of the General Council [of the First International] to the Fourth Annual Congress of the International Working Men's Association," published as a pamphlet, September, 1869*

... A FEW WEEKS after the meeting of our last Congress, a memorable strike on the part of the ribbon weavers and silk dyers occurred in Basel, a place which to our days has conserved much of the features of a medieval town with its local traditions, its narrow prejudices, its purse-proud patricians, and its patriarchal rule of the employer over the employed. Still, a few years ago a Basel manufacturer boasted to an English secretary of embassy that "the position of the master and the man was on a better footing here than in England," that "in Switzerland the operative who leaves a good master for better wages would be despised by his own fellow workmen," and that "our advantage lies principally in the length of the working time and the moderation of the wages." You see, patriarchalism, as modified by modern influences, comes to this—that the master is good, and that his wages are bad, that the laborer feels like a medieval vassal, and is exploited like a modern wage slave.

This patriarchalism may further be appreciated from an official Swiss inquiry into the factory employment of children and the state of the primary public schools. It was ascertained that "the Basel school atmosphere is the worst in the world, that while in the free air carbonic acid forms only 4 parts of 10,000, and in closed rooms should not exceed 10 parts, it rose in Basel common schools to 20–81 parts in the

---

* Text in *Karl Marx on the First International*, Vol. III of the Karl Marx Library, pp. 37–38.

forenoon, and to 53–94 in the afternoon." Thereupon a member of the Basel Great Council, Mr. Thurneysen, coolly replied, "Don't allow yourselves to be frightened. The parents have passed through school-rooms as bad as the present ones, and yet they have escaped with their skins safe."

The Women of Paris (I)

From *The Civil War in France* (1871)*

THE WOMEN OF PARIS joyfully give up their lives at the barricades and on the place of execution. What does this prove? Why, that the demon of the Commune has changed them into Megaeras and Hecates!

* For text, see *Karl Marx on Revolution*, Vol. I. of The Karl Marx Library, p. 365.

(II)

From *The Civil War in France* (1871)*

THE COCOTTES had refound the scent of their protectors—the absconding men of family, religion, and, above all, of property. In their stead, the real women of Paris showed again at the surface—heroic, noble, and devoted, like the women of antiquity. Working, thinking, fighting, bleeding Paris—almost forgetful, in its incubation of a new society, of the cannibals at its gates—radiant in their enthusiasm of its historic initiative!

* For text, see *Karl Marx on Revolution*, Vol. I of The Karl Marx Library, p. 358.

Female and Child Labor

From "Marginal Notes to the Program of the German Workers' Party"
(Gotha Program) (1875), Part IV

3. Restriction of Female Labor and Prohibition of Child Labor

THE STANDARDIZATION of the working day must include the restriction of female labor, insofar as it relates to the duration, intermissions, etc., of the working day; otherwise it could only mean the exclusion of female labor from branches of industry that are especially unhealthy for the female body or are objectionable morally for the female sex. If that is what was meant, it should so have been said.

"Prohibition of child labor." Here it was absolutely essential to state the age limit.

A general prohibition of child labor is incompatible with the existence of large-scale industry and hence an empty, pious wish. Its realization—if it were possible—would be reactionary, since, with a strict regulation of the working time according to the different age groups and other safety measures for the protection of children, an early combination of productive labor with education is one of the most potent means for the transformation of present-day society.

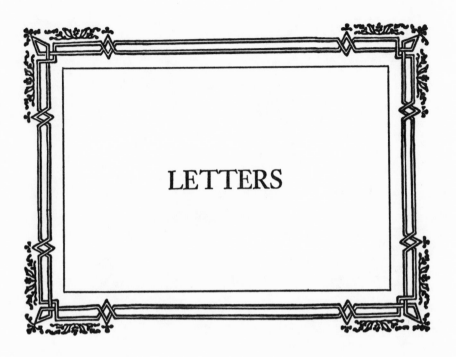

LETTERS

Postscripts to letter to Adolf Cluss (*in Washington*)
LONDON, OCTOBER 8, 1852

Notabene. The little erudition that the unfortunate Heinzen, whose ignorance is well known, has conspicuously displayed in his account of the historic development of marriage, he copied from G. Jung, *History of Women*, Part I, Frankfurt, 1850.[1] Jung himself took his materials from:

C. Meiners, *History of the Female Sex*, 4 vols., Hanover, 1788–1800;[2] and from:

J. A. de Ségur, *The Women*, etc., 3 vols., Paris, 1803,[3] and poured on it Young German Hegelian sauce.

Meiners and Ségur used:

W. Alexander, *History of Women*, etc., 2 vols., London, 1782, 3d ed.

Thomas (of the French Academy), *Essays on the Character*, etc., *of Women*, etc., Paris, 1773.[4]

Finally, for the Hegelian conception—the old rascal-fool Ruge, who is entirely childish, is too stupid to count—see:

J. Unger, *Marriage in its World Historical Development*, Vienna, 1850.

With this "bibliography" you can drive away the unfortunate Heinzen's inclination to present a few phrases snapped up from the

---

1. Georg Jung, *Geschichte der Frauen.*
2. Christoph Meiners, *Geschichte des weiblichen Geschlechts.*
3. Joseph-Alexandre de Ségur, *Les Femmes, leur condition et leur influence dans l'ordre social chez différents peuples anciens et modernes.*
4. Antoine-Léonard Thomas, *Essai sur le caractère, les mœurs et l'esprit des femmes dans les différent siècles.*

socialists as a new discovery, and give the German-American public the sources in which to find the material, if it is interested.

Letter to Mrs. Jenny Marx (in London)
MANCHESTER, JUNE 21, 1856

My heart's beloved:

I am writing you again because I am alone and because it troubles me always to have a dialogue with you in my head, without your knowing anything about it or hearing it or being able to answer. Poor as your portrait is, it does perform a service for me, and I now understand how even the "black Madonna," the most disgraceful portrait of the Mother of God, could find indestructible admirers, indeed even more admirers than the good portraits. In any case, those black Madonna pictures have never been more kissed, looked at, and adored than your photograph, which, although not black, is morose, and absolutely does not reflect your darling, sweet, kissable "*dolce*" face. But I improve upon the sun's rays, which have painted falsely, and find that my eyes, so spoiled by lamplight and tobacco, can still paint, not only in a dream but also while awake. I have you vivaciously before me, and I carry you on my hands, and I kiss you from head to foot, and I fall on my knees before you, and I groan: "Madame, I love you." And I truly love you, more than the Moor of Venice ever loved. The false and worthless world views virtually all [literary] characters falsely and worthlessly. Who of my many slanderers and snake-tongued enemies have ever accused me of being destined to play the role of chief lover in a second class theater? And yet it is true. If the scoundrels had had wit, they would have painted "the production and direction" on one side, and me lying at your feet on the other. Look to this picture and to that[1]—they would have written underneath. But dumb scoundrels they are and dumb they will remain, *in seculum seculorum.*

Momentary absence is good, for in constant presence things seem too much alike to be differentiated. Proximity dwarfs even towers, while the petty and the commonplace, at close view, grow too big. Small habits, which may physically irritate and take on emotional form, disappear when the immediate object is removed from the eye. Great passions, which through proximity assume the form of petty routine, grow and again take on their natural dimension through the magic of distance. So it is with my love. You have only to be snatched away from me even in a mere dream, and I know immediately that the time

---

1. These seven words were written by Marx in English.

has only served, as do sun and rain for plants, for growth. The moment you are absent, my love for you shows itself to be what it is, a giant, in which are crowded together all the energy of my spirit and all the character of my heart. It makes me feel like a man again, because I feel a great passion; and the multifariousness, in which study and modern education entangle us, and the skepticism which necessarily makes us find fault with all subjective and objective impressions, all of these are entirely designed to make us all small and weak and whining. But love— not love for the Feuerbach-type of man, not for the metabolism, not for the proletariat—but the love for the beloved and particularly for you, makes a man again a man.

You will smile, my sweet, and ask, how did I come to all this rhetoric? If I could press your sweet, white heart to my heart, I would keep silent and not say a word. Since I cannot kiss with my lips, I must kiss with language and make words. I could really even make verses and rhymes like Ovid's *Libri Tristium*, which in German means *Buecher des Jammers* [Books of Laments]. But I am exiled from you, which is something Ovid did not conceive.

There are actually many females in the world, and some among them are beautiful. But where could I find again a face whose every feature, even every wrinkle, is a reminder of the greatest and sweetest memories of my life? Even my endless pains, my irreplaceable losses[2] I read in your sweet countenance, and I kiss away the pain when I kiss your sweet face. "Buried in her arms, awakened by her kisses"— namely, in your arms and by your kisses, and I grant the Brahmins and Pythagoras their doctrine of regeneration and Christianity its doctrine of resurrection. . . .

Good-bye, my sweet heart. I kiss you and the children many thousand times.

Yours,
KARL

From letter to Frederick Engels (in Manchester)
LONDON, DECEMBER 11, 1858

Dear Engels:
. . . Here in the house it looks "more dreary and desolate out than ever."[1] Since my wife herself cannot prepare a Christmas celebration

---

2. Marx refers to the death of their three young children: Guido, Franziska, and Edgar.

---

1. The words in quotation marks were written by Marx in English.

for the children, and, instead, is being hounded from all sides with debt-reminder notes and is also copying the manuscript,[2] and in between has to run to the pawnshops in the City, the mood here is extraordinarily dismal. Withal, my wife is quite right when she says that after all this misery that she has had to go through it will become worse after the revolution when she will have the dubious pleasure of seeing all the local humbugs again celebrating triumphs over yonder. Women are like that. And the feminine behavior of the Freiligraths, etc., and other acquaintances rightly embitter her. She says *à la guerre comme à la guerre*.[3] But there is no *guerre*. Everything is bourgeois.
    Salut.   *Yours,*

                                                                K.M.

From letter to Lion Philips (*in Zalt-Bommel*)
LONDON, MAY 6, 1861

Dear Uncle:
    ... You will recall, dear Uncle, how often we joked about the fact that nowadays the breeding of men is so much behind the breeding of cattle. Now I have seen your whole family and must declare you to be a *virtuoso in human breeding*. I have never in my life known a better family. All your children are independent characters, each one a personality, each possesses his own intellectual qualities, and all are also marked by humane culture. ...

                                                    Your devoted nephew,

                                                                K. MARX

From letter to Frederick Engels (*in Manchester*)
LONDON, MAY 1, 1865

Dear Fred!
    ... Today is Jennychen's birthday, and this evening I will have Ernest Jones,[1] together with Odger,[2] Cremer,[3] Fox,[4] and Jung,[5] in

---

2. *Critique of Political Economy*, published in 1859.
3. War is war.

---

1. Ernest Charles Jones (1819–1869), a Chartist leader and friend of Marx.
2. George Odger (1820–1877), an English shoemaker, member of the International.

my house, so that the birthday will be celebrated politically. Laura had "the question popped" by a certain Charles Manning, a native South American, whose father is English and mother Spanish. He is rich and otherwise a decent fellow, but Laura "does not care a pin for him." The Southern passion "she has already known how to damp."[6] But since his sisters are acquainted with my girls, and he is frightfully in love, it is a disagreeable case. . . .

Yours,
K.M.

From letter written in French to Paul Lafargue (*in London*)
LONDON, AUGUST 13, 1866

My dear Lafargue:

Permit me the following observations:

1. If you want to continue contact with my daughter [Laura], you must give up your manner of "paying court" to her. You know well that there is as yet no promise of marriage, that it is still up in the air.[1] And even if you were formally her betrothed, you must not forget that a lengthy business is involved here. The habits of all too intimate relationship are even more inappropriate here in that both lovers will have to live in chastity in the same place for a necessarily prolonged period under strong temptations. In the course of a geologic era of a single week, I have observed with shock the change in your conduct. In my opinion, true love is expressed in reserve, modesty, and even shyness of the lover toward his idol, and never in temperamental excesses or too premature intimacy. When you invoke your Creole temperament, then I consider it my duty to step in between your temperament and my daughter with my healthy common sense. If you are unable to show your love for her in the form consonant with the London latitude, then it is advisable that you love her from a distance. I don't have to elaborate further.

2. Before your relations with Laura are definitely settled, I must be completely clear about your economic circumstances. My daughter

---

3. William Randall Cremer (1838–1908), an English carpenter, member of the International.

4. Peter Fox (d. 1869), an English journalist, member of the International.

5. Hermann Jung (1830–1901), a German refugee watchmaker in London, member of the International.

6. The words in quotation marks were written by Marx in English.

---

1. See Marx's letter to Engels, August 7, 1866.

believes that I know about your affairs. She is mistaken. I have not talked about these things because it is my opinion that it was your duty to take the initiative. You know that I have sacrificed my whole fortune to the revolutionary struggle. I do not regret it. Quite the contrary. If I had to start my life over again, I would do the same. But I would not marry. Insofar as it is in my power, I want to protect my daughter from the kind of rocks on which her mother's life has been wrecked. Since this affair would never have reached this stage without my inaction (a weakness on my part!) and without the influence that my friendship for you had on my daughter's attitude, a heavy personal responsibility rests upon me. In regard to your present circumstances, the information, which I did not seek but received only accidentally, is not reassuring. But let us leave that. As for your general position, I know that you are still a student, that on account of the Liège event[2] your career in France is half wrecked, that you still lack the English language—an indispensable condition for your acclimatization in England—and that your chances are at best altogether problematical. Observation has proved to me that you are not diligent by nature, despite occasional feverish activity and good intentions. Under these circumstances, you are destined to depend upon others to help in your making a common life with my daughter. I know nothing about your family. Even if they live in prosperous circumstances, it does not prove that they are willing to bear sacrifices for you. I do not even know how they feel about your proposed marriage. It is necessary for me, I repeat, to have a positive clarification of all these questions.[3] For the rest, a professed realist like you cannot expect that I should behave like an idealist where the future of my daughter is concerned. A positive person like you, one who wants to abolish poverty, would not want to make poverty at the expense of my child.

3. In order to anticipate every false interpretation of this letter, I call your attention to the fact that—should you feel tempted to enter into the marriage today—you will not succeed. My daughter would refuse. I would protest. You ought to have achieved something in life before you can think of marriage, and this will require a long testing period for you and Laura.

4. I would appreciate it if this letter remained between us. I await your reply.

Entirely yours,
KARL MARX

---

2. In October 1865, Lafargue attended an international student congress in Liège, for which he and other students were suspended from French universities.
3. See Marx's letter to Engels, August 23, 1866, on Lafargue's father's acceptance of Laura as Paul's bride.

Karl Marx, letter to Frederick Engels (*in Manchester*)
LONDON, AUGUST 23, 1866

Dear Fred:

Today, only a few words. The matter with Lafargue[1] is arranged to the extent that the Old Man[2] wrote me from Bordeaux, asking me for the title of *promesso sposo* [betrothed] for his son and stating his very favorable economic circumstances. Apart from that, it is agreed that Lafargue *jeune* [the younger] must take his doctoral examination in London and then in Paris before he can think of marrying. So far the thing is settled. But yesterday I informed our Creole that if he cannot calm himself down to English manners, Laura will give him his congé without further ado. This he must fully realize, or nothing will come of the thing. He is an extremely good chap, but an *enfant gâté* [spoiled child] and too much a child of nature.

Laura states that before she becomes engaged formally, she must have your consent.

Here and there I have the beginnings of new carbuncles, which keep on disappearing, but they force me to keep my working hours within limits.

Best regards for Lizzy.

Greetings.

Yours,

K.M.

Letter written in English to Laura Marx (*in Hastings*)
LONDON, AUGUST 28, 1866

My dear Cacadou:

I have received your letter, but not unopened, since it had to pass through the fingered hands of the Emperor.[1]

It was always my opinion that to give the last finishing stroke to your "heducation," some sort of boarding school training was still wanted. It will do you a great deal of good.

Il hidalgo della figura trista[2] left me at the corner of his house. His

---

1. See Marx's letter to Engels, August 13, 1866.
2. François Lafargue (d. 1870 or 1871), Paul Lafargue's father.

---

1. Marx's daughter Jenny, whose nickname was "Emperor of China," acting as his secretary. All the Marx children had various nicknames.
2. Paul Lafargue, born in Santiago, Cuba, became engaged to Laura Marx on August 6. "The knight of the rueful countenance" is Don Quixote.

heart having been considerably shaken before, he seemed to bear his separation *from me* with a rather heroic indifference.

My best wishes to ±○○╪.[3]

I enclose 5 £, the remainder to be sent in the second week.

Yours humbly,

OLD ONE

Mama will start upon her own expedition tomorrow or the day after tomorrow. A great push was wanted to set her amoving.

From letter to Ludwig Kugelmann (*in Hanover*)
LONDON, JUNE 10, 1867

Dear Friend:

... The crossing from Hamburg to London, apart from a bit of rough weather on the first day, was generally favorable. A few hours before arrival at London, a German girl, whose military bearing had already struck me, declared that she wanted that same evening to go from London to Weston supra Mare and did not know how she would manage it with her many pieces of luggage. The matter was the worse in that on the Sabbath day helpful hands are in short supply in England. Friends had warned her about it in a postal card. She had to go to the North Western Station, which I also had to pass. As a good knight, I, therefore, offered to drop her off there. She accepted. Thinking it over, it occurred to me, however, that Weston supra Mare is to the southwest, while the station which I was to pass and to which she was going was in the northwest. I consulted the sea captain. Correct. It turned out that she was to be let off at a station at the opposite end of London from my direction. But I had made the promise, and now I had to make *bonne mine à mauvais jeu* [put a good face on it]. We arrived at 2 o'clock in the afternoon. I brought *la donna errante* [lady errant] to her station, where I learned that her train would not leave until 8 in the evening. So I was in for it,[1] and had to kill six hours walking in Hyde Park, sitting in ice-shops, etc. It turned out that her name was Elisabeth von Puttkammer, Bismarck's niece, with whom she had just spent a few weeks in Berlin. She had the whole Army roster with her, as her family supplies our "brave Army" with Gentlemen of Honor and *Taille* in superabundance. She was a gay, educated girl, but aristocratic and black-and-white [the colors of the royal flag] to the tip of her nose. She was not a little surprised to dis-

---

3. Laura.

---

1. These 6 words were written in English.

cover that she had fallen into "red" hands. I consoled her, however, that our rendezvous would end "without bloodshed," and I saw her depart for her destination *saine et sauve* [safe and sound]. Think what food this would supply to Blind[2] and other vulgar democrats—my conspiracy with Bismarck! . . .

Yours,
KARL MARX

From letter to Frederick Engels (*in Manchester*)
LONDON, NOVEMBER 7, 1867

Dear Fred:
. . . The old Urquhart[1] with his Catholicism, etc., grows more and more disgusting.

On lit dans un registre d'une inquisition d'Italie cet aveu d'une religieuse; elle disait innocemment à la Madonne: "De grace, sainte Vierge, donne moi quelqu'un avec qui je puisse pécher."[2] In this respect, too, the Russians are stronger. It has been established that a thoroughly healthy chap who spent only twenty-four hours in a Russian nunnery came out dead. The nuns rode him to death. Of course, their father confessor does *not enter* every day.

From postscript to letter to Frederick Engels (*in Manchester*)
LONDON, SEPTEMBER 25, 1868

Dear Fred:
. . . In a Blue Book on the crisis of 1857, Cardwell, Chairman of the Investigating Committee, asked Dixon (managing director of a bankrupt Liverpool bank), the disgusting washerwoman among the Peelite old wives' clique, if the shareholders of the bank consisted mostly of women, parsons, and other persons without insight into the banking system. By no means, replies Dixon, they were mostly *"mercantile men,"* but added very knowingly:

---

2. Karl Blind, a German refugee journalist in London, enemy of Marx.

---

1. David Urquhart (1805–1877), a British diplomat and Tory member of Parliament.
2. One reads in an Italian Inquisition record the following avowal of a nun, who innocently prays to the Madonna: "I beseech you, Holy Virgin, give me somebody with whom I could sin."

"The majority of them are people in business, mercantile men; but how far mercantile men can be considered competent to form an opinion *on any other business than their own,* is *rather* a question." Is this not charming?

Postscript to letter to Ludwig Kugelmann (*in Hanover*)
LONDON, DECEMBER 5, 1868

Is your wife also active in the great German women's emancipation campaign? I believe that German women must begin by driving their husbands to self-emancipation.[1]

From letter to Ludwig Kugelmann (*in Hanover*)
LONDON, DECEMBER 12, 1868

Dear Friend:
    ... Tell your wife I never "suspected" her of serving under Lady-General Geck.[1] My question was only a joke. In any case, ladies cannot complain about the "International," for it has elected a lady, Madame Law,[2] to membership in the General Council. Joking aside, great progress was shown in the last congress of the American Labor Union,[3] which, among other things, treated working women with complete equality, while in this respect the English, and still more the gallant French, are burdened with a narrow-minded spirit. Anybody who knows anything of history also knows that great social changes are impossible without the female ferment. Social progress can be measured accurately by the social status of the beautiful sex (the ugly ones included). . . .
    With best regards,   *Yours,*
                                                                        K.M.

---

1. See also Marx's letter to Kugelmann, December 12, 1868.

---

1. Marie Goegg (b. 1826), chairman of the women's section of the International.
2. Harriet Law, an English feminist and atheist.
3. The National Labor Union, founded in Baltimore in August 1866.

Letter written in French to François Lafargue[1] (in Bordeaux)
PARIS, JULY 10, 1869

My dear Friend:

I arrived here Thursday evening [July 8][2] and will return to London on Monday [July 12].

Judging from your letter, which I have reread, you seem to assume that my wife is still here. This is an error.

I have been particularly shocked by the fact that Laura is still suffering and that her health has been very much affected.

I begin with this, because it explains the seeming indifference of our Paul. He has not interrupted his studies, but only postponed them, in order to take the necessary steps for his examinations.

To the reproaches which I have made him, he replied, and I must admit rightly so: "Before I can think of the future, I have to take care of the present. Laura's state of health requires my most anxious care. It does not even allow me to stay out for any length of time. I wanted to keep the situation secret, in order not to worry her and my family. Laura and I did everything not to arouse Frau Marx's suspicions."

I have spoken to a very good doctor, who visits Paul's home. He told me that Laura absolutely must go to the seashore, and he recommended Dieppe, because a longer trip would affect her health.

In addition, Paul promised me that after his return from Dieppe he would do his best to shorten the time, etc., for his doctor's examination.

I must tell you candidly that my daughter's state of health alarms me seriously.

Our grandchild[3] is an enchanting youngster. I have never seen such a beautifully shaped child's head.

My compliments to your wife.

Accept, my dear friend, the heartiest regards from

Yours,

KARL MARX

---

1. François Lafargue (d. 1870 or 1871), father of Paul Lafargue.
2. See Marx's letter to Engels, July 14, 1869, in which he says that he arrived in Paris on Tuesday, July 6.
3. Charles-Étienne Lafargue, born in 1868, died at the age of four in 1872.

From letter to Frederick Engels (in Manchester)
LONDON, JULY 22, 1869

Dear Fred:

... I have had another "family" unpleasantness. For some time now I have noticed that my wife does not make ends meet with the money I give her weekly, although our expenses have not increased in any way. Since I absolutely do not want to get into debt again, and since the money I gave her last Monday was "all gone" today [Thursday], I asked for an explanation. Then the folly of women came out. In the list of debts which she had drawn up for you,[1] she had concealed about £75, which she has been trying to pay off by and by from her household allowance. I asked, why this? Reply: She was afraid to tell me about such a big sum! Women obviously always need a guardian! ...[2]

Greetings.   *Yours,*
                                                         KARL MARX

Letter (written in English) to Laura Lafargue (in London)
HANOVER, SEPTEMBER 25, 1869

My dear Cacadou:

I regret that I cannot celebrate at home the birthday of my dear bird's eye, but Old Nick's thoughts are with you.

Du bist beslôzen
in mînem Herzen.[1]

I was happy to see from Möhmchen's[2] letter (written in her usual amusing way, she is a real virtuoso in letter writing) that your health is improving. Our dear little Schnappy[3] will, I hope, soon get better.

---

1. See Engels letter to Marx, November 29, 1868.
2. Engels to Marx, July 25, 1869: "As for the £75, don't let it cause you any gray hairs; as soon as Gottfried [Ermen] has paid me my next installment . . . I will send it to you. Only see to it that this does not happen again in the future; you know that our estimates have been tightly calculated, leaving absolutely no margin for extravagances."
Marx to Engels, August 4, 1869: "Dear Fred: the £100 received with best thanks. I shall now watch the proceedings so closely that similar mistakes, etc."

1. From a medieval (A.D. 1200) folk song; the words mean: "Thou art locked in my heart."
2. Mrs. Karl Marx: the word is a diminutive for "mother."
3. Charles-Étienne Lafargue (1868–1872), Marx's grandson.

At the same time, I fully share Kugelmann's opinion that Dr. West[4] ought to be consulted at once (or another medical man if he be absent).

I trust you and Lafargue will in this case yield to my paternal authority, a thing, you know full well, I am not in the habit of invoking. Nobody is more difficult to treat than a baby. In no case more immediate action is wanted, and any delay more hurtful. You must under no circumstances accelerate your departure from London. It would be really dangerous to the child and do no good to yourself. On this point, every medical man will give you the same advice.

I am glad the Basel congress is over, and has, comparatively speaking, gone so well. I am always fretting on such occasions of public exhibition of the party *mit allen ihren Geschwüren* [with all its ulcers]. None of the actors was *à la hauteur des principes* [up to high principles], but the higher-class idiocy effaces the working-class blunders. We have passed through no little German town the *Winkelblatt* [local newspaper] of which was not full of the doings of "that formidable Congress."

We are here in a sort of fix. The Kugelmanns will not hear of an early leavetaking. At the same time, Jenny is much improving in health consequent upon the change of air and circumstances. With Liebknecht I am likely to meet, within a few days, at Braunschweig [Brunswick]. I decline going to Leipzig, and he cannot come to Hanover, since the Prussians would probably give him the advantages of free lodging during the present prorogation of the Reichstag.

My best thanks to Paul for his elaborate letter. *Meine herzlichsten Grüsse an das ganze Haus* [My heartiest regards to the whole house] and hundred kisses to yourself and my dear little Schnappy.

Adio, dear child.

> *Ever yours,*
> OLD NICK *

From letter to Frederick Engels (in Manchester)
LONDON, MAY 11, 1870

Dear Fred:

. . . In regard to the Welsh,[1] I do not find the main subject in my notebooks. But here are some notes:

---

* His children's nickname for Marx.
4. Charles West (1816–1898), a London children's specialist.

---

1. Engels to Marx, May 11, 1870: "Can you put together for me a note, with sources, on the Welsh phanerogamic system? I can use it just now, to write about it in the next few days."

"Communal property went out with the loosening of the marriage bond, but at the same time there was the *women's right to vote* in the tribal assembly" (W. Wachsmuth, *Europaeische Sittengeschichte*, Part II, Leipzig, 1833).

Wachsmuth bases his statement on the laws of Kings Dyonwall Moelmud and Howel Ddas. *Leges Molmutinae* (translated by William Probert): *The ancient laws of Cambria*, containing the institutional triads of D. Moelmud, the laws of Howel the Good, triadical commentaries, code of education, and the hunting laws of Wales (London, 1823); and Edward Davies, *Celtic Researches* (London, 1804).

I find these curiosa in my notebooks:

"Statutes on the testing of virginity. An individual's testimony suffices; for example: the girl's statement about her own virginity."

"A man who repudiates his bedmate in favor of another has to pay a fine of enough denarii to cover the plaintiff's behind. A woman who accuses a man of rape swears out her deposition by seizing his penis with her left hand and placing her right hand on a reliquary."

"*Lewdness with the Queen* cost double *mult* [fine] to the king."

The first chapter of the book on the civil code deals with women. "If a wife sleeps with another man and *he beats her*, he [the husband] loses his claims for compensation. . . . What the woman may sell [alienate]—depending upon her status is clearly stated. The wife of a peasant (*taenigh*) may sell only her necklace and *hide* only the sieve, and ask for their return only within the reach of her voice. The wife of a nobleman (*nihelms*) may sell coat, shirt, shoes, etc., and *hide* the whole household stuff. *For the woman, sufficient grounds for divorce* were the husband's impotence, body scabs, and *bad breath*."

Very gallant fellows, those Celts! Also born dialecticians, because everything is constructed in *triads*. As for phanerogamy, as soon as I am able to leave the house I will look up Wachsmuth in the British Museum. . . .

Yours,

K.M.

Letter written in English to Paul Lafargue (in Bordeaux)
LONDON, FEBRUARY 4, 1871

Dear Paul:

Il faut créer des nouveaux défenseurs à la France.[1] You and Laura seem seriously and successfully engaged in that patriotic business. The

---

1. "It is necessary to produce new defenders of France." The reference is to Laura Lafargue's third child, a boy, who died later, on July 26, 1871.

whole family was delighted to hear that our dear Laura has passed victoriously through the critical juncture and we hope the progress will prove no less favorable. Embrace little Schnappy on my part and tell him that Old Nick feels highly elated at the two photograms of his successor. In the "serious" copy the stern qualities of the little man protrude, while in his attitude as *franc-fileur*[2] there is a charming expression of humor and *espièglerie* [roguishness]....

Yours,

OLD NICK

From letter to Laura Lafargue (in Madrid)
LONDON, FEBRUARY 28, 1872

My dear child:

You may judge of the overwork[1] I am being bothered with ever since December last from my negligence in replying to your own and Paul's letters. Still my heart was always with you. In fact, the health of poor little Schnappy[2] occupies my thoughts more than everything else, and I feel even a little angry at Paul's last epistle, full of interesting details as to the "movement," but a mere blank in regard to that dear little sufferer....

And now, my dear child, adio, with thousand kisses for little Schnappy and yourself, and my greetings to Paul.

Yours most devotedly,

OLD NICK

---

2. *Franc-fileur* was the epithet applied to those who fled from Paris during the siege. Laura called her infant son a *franc-fileur* because he was frightened of unaccustomed things.

---

1. Marx was busy preparing the second German edition of *Capital,* as well as organizing the last congress of the First International, which met in The Hague, September 2–7.

2. Schnappy was the nickname of Marx's grandson, Charles-Étienne Lafargue, who died in July 1872, at the age of four.

From letter to Frederick Engels (*in Ramsgate*)
LONDON, AUGUST 14, 1874

Dear Fred:

. . . Tussy[1] feels much better; her appetite grows in geometric proportion, but this is peculiar to these feminine sicknesses[2] where the hysterical plays a role; one has to act as if one does not notice that she again lives on terrestrial nourishment. But this too will disappear as soon as there is complete recovery. . . .

Yours,
K.M.

From letter to Jenny Longuet (*in Malvern*)
LONDON, SEPTEMBER 16, 1878

My dear child:

I hope that the better reports about Johnny[1] continue. You must send me bulletins every day and always the exact truth. The little man is the apple of my eye. Above all he must be treated indulgently, hence not too much movement (passive or active) out of his home. If he continues to make progress, as I hope, it would perhaps be better to leave Saturday[2] (instead of Friday). For another day of rest and recovery is very important in his case. . . .

Yours,
MOHR

---

1. Marx's youngest daughter, Eleanor.
2. Eleanor was pining from love for Prosper-Olivier Lissagaray, a French journalist; Marx disapproved of the relationship.

---

1. Jean-Laurent-Frederick (Johnny) Longuet, Marx's two-year-old grandson.
2. September 21.

*Letter written in German, French, and English to Jenny Longuet
(in Ramsgate)*
ST. HILIERS, AUGUST 19, 1879

My darling beloved Jennychen:

Hurrah for the little world citizen![1] Il faut peupler le monde de garçons d'autant plus que la statistique anglaise montre un excès de filles.[2] I am glad that the catastrophe [the delivery] has come off happily, alas under difficult conditions. The arrangement which Mamma has made seems to me far from the most convenient. At all events, Tussy and myself leave tomorrow for London and then I shall be very soon *at your side* and everything will be quietly settled. Here the rainy time—otherwise so unknown to this delicious island—has again set in, so that we had already commenced discussing our departure, the whole aspect of our sojourn here having changed with the climatic and meteorologic changes. The Hôtel de l'Europe is excellent and one day we must go here together, toute la famille [the whole family].

I can hardly expect tomorrow morning when the boat will start from here to Southampton. I feel so anxious with you and little Johnny.

In the meantime my best compliments to Mamma and Longuet. Don't fret or worry or become melancholy, my Child, everything will be all right.

Your faithful,

OLD NICK

You must excuse the brevity of these lines, as the letter has to be mailed immediately.

---

1. On August 18, 1879, Jenny Longuet gave birth to a boy, Edgar, in Ramsgate.
2. It is necessary to populate the world with boys, the more so as English statistics show an excess of girls.

From letter to Jenny Longuet (in Argenteuil)
LONDON, APRIL 29, 1881

My dear Jenny:

I congratulate you on the happy delivery;[1] at least I assume that everything is in order, as you took the trouble to write yourself. My "women" expected that the "new earth citizen" would increase "the better half" of the population; personally, I prefer the "male" sex among children who will be born at this turning point in history. They have before them the most revolutionary period that men have ever experienced. It is bad nowadays to be so "old" as to have to foresee instead of see. . . .

Yours,

OLD NICK

From letters written in English by Laura Lafargue to Frederick Engels (in London)
PARIS, JUNE 20, 1883

My dear General:

. . . I requested you, the other day, to inform me (which as you had made a public declaration, I had a right to do) whether Mohr[1] had told *you* that he wished Tussy[2] to be his literary executrix. You have not answered me. Had you answered in the affirmative I should have simply concluded that long illness had much changed my dear father and should not have loved and honoured him one bit the less for that!

Papa, in health, would not have made of his *eldest and favorite daughter*[3] his sole literary executrix, to the exclusion of his other daughters—he had too great a love of equality for that—let alone the last of his daughters.[4] Thus much I know. As to what the world thinks and says, I, who am my father's and my mother's second daughter, don't care one straw!

Yours, my dear General, Most affectionately.   [no signature]

---

1. Marcel Longuet, Marx's grandson, who lived into the middle of the twentieth century, dying in 1949.

---

1. Marx's nickname among members of his family and close friends.
2. Eleanor, Marx's youngest daughter.
3. Jenny Longuet.
4. Eleanor Marx.

INDEX

Accidents, labor, 83, 123
Adultery, 58, 59
Advertiser (London), 76
Agricultural Workers, 106, 114n
  (*See also* Peasants)
Agriculture, 109
Alexander, William, 135
America (*see* United States)
American education, 33
Americans, 86
Anglican Church (*see* Church of
  England)
Annenkov, Pavel V., xi
Apparel industry, 108–110, 119n
Apprentices, apprenticeships, 34, 89–
  90, 94, 113
  (*See also* Child labor; Domestic
  industry; Handicrafts)
Aristotle, xx, 14
Arkwright, Sir Richard, 117
Army, 37
Art, 8, 13
Asylums and Poor Houses, 78 & n,
  80
Atheism, 34
  (*See also* Religion)
Aveling, Edward, 93

Bacon, Sir Francis, 14 & n
Ballard, Dr. Edward, 107

Barracks, 105
Barrot, Camille, 26n
Basel, 127–128
  (*See also* Switzerland)
Bauer, Bruno, 15
Bawdiness, xvii–xxi
  (*See also* Sex)
Beauty, 49
Bee-Hive (London), 35n
Beggary (*see* Pauperism)
Belgium, 101
Berlin, University of, xxi
Bellers, John, 117n
Bismarck, Otto von, 41n, 142
Blacks (*see* Negroes)
Blackstone, Sir William, 57
Blanc, Louis, 27
Blanqui, Louis Auguste, 27
Blind, Karl, 143 & n
Blue Books (*see* Factory Inspectors'
  Reports)
Boehme, Jakob, xvi
Boerne, Ludwig, 49n, 66
Boileau, Étienne, 114n
Bourgeois, bourgeoisie, xii, xiii, xvi,
  xxvi, 18, 23, 25, 27, 41, 61, 64, 66,
  67–68, 95, 115n, 138
Bourgeois wife, 68
Boys, preference for, 151 & n, 152
  workers (*see* Child labor)